Scribe Publications
TERROR

Dr John Carroll has degrees in mathematics, economics, and sociology from the universities of Melbourne and Cambridge, and is reader in sociology at La Trobe University in Melbourne. The author of numerous books, and a frequent writer of essays and newspaper articles, he delivered one of the Alfred Deakin Federation Lectures in 2001. His work focuses on modern Western society, and in particular on the forces that alternatively hold it together and press it towards disintegration.

TERROR

A MEDITATION ON THE MEANING OF SEPTEMBER 11

John Carroll

Scribe Publications

Melbourne

Scribe Publications Pty Ltd
PO Box 523
Carlton North, Victoria, Australia 3054
Email: scribe@bigpond.net.au

First published by Scribe Publications 2002

Typeset in 11.5 on 15 pt Berthold Bodoni by the publisher
Cover design by Miriam Rosenbloom
Printed and bound in Australia by Griffin Press

National Library of Australia
Cataloguing-in-Publication data

Carroll, John, 1944- .
Terror : a meditation on the meaning of September 11.

ISBN 0 908011 84 9
1. September 11 Terrorist Attacks, 2001. 2. Terrorism. 3.
Civilization, Modern - 21st century. 4. Social values. I.
Title.

303.372

www.scribepub.com.au

CONTENTS

1 THE NEW DAWN

The hijacked planes were flown through the bright, early-morning, American east-coast sky. This is the hour of Apollo, the sun god, who presided over ancient Delphi. His oracle dwelt high on the side of the sacred mountain, with two mottos carved over its portal. Two sayings watched over the foundation of our civilization, in exhortation and warning: 'Know Thyself!' and 'Nothing Too Much!'

Ignorantly and flagrantly, the modern West has violated both. It has turned its back on its ancestral wisdom. Yet the Delphic god, while bathed in light, looks down with a cool and detached eye, contemptuous. His is not the heated way of the ancient Hebrew prophet storming in from the desert to rant at wayward humanity: 'Sinners repent, or be damned!' His concern is not with moral corruption, but with a lack of fidelity to the truth—the truth about *being*—and excess. Apollo's concern is with a metaphysical condition. It is for this that the modern West is being brought to judgment.

We all know the story — about the events of September 11, 2001 and their aftermath. We all share the shock, surreal image of the second plane slicing through the World Trade Center tower like a knife through butter. We will take to our graves the slow-motion horror of watching, many of us as it happened, the tallest skyscrapers in the world crumpling, one after the other — each no more substantial than a child's house of cards. Nothing was left of where 50,000 people had once worked but dust and smoke, numb pain for those trapped inside, and speechless awe at the power that had done this.

These, however, are the surface facts. The heart of the matter lies deep beneath. This is a story that is hard to read, essential to read. The foundations of the modern West shake. September 11, 2001 may mark an end, and a beginning that no one would choose — so point the obscure early clues. The half-century Golden Age that ran from 1950 to the start of the millennium may be over. It is possible that the American era may itself have had its end triggered, and with it the supremacy of the West, of what it stands for and what it stands on. Everything depends on the inner response.

The inner response, to be right, this time needs guidance. Self-examination — with clarity, single-minded intent, and endurance — will prove an ordeal for a culture that has become complacent and comfortable. The modern West is heavily draped in tactics for inducing oblivion, so as not to know, so as to restore the pretence that all is well and that this half-hearted waddle through the days is living—believing that central heating, hamburgers, and sitcoms are enough to anchor existence.

Our culture has developed the shrug of the shoulders into a cosy reflex while we pour another drink, switch on the amusement parade, and wait for house prices and the stock market to rise. Will this culture be able to relearn how to take itself seriously? Will it be able to dispel the deep, ingrained cynicism that its leaders are papier-mâché dolls, egos without a scintilla of vision beyond their own petty wishes, beyond their own craving for power, money, and celebrity? Will it be able to believe, in its viscera, in the rhetoric from the top about our great nation and its fortitude, in the decency of its people, in its will to bring justice? Will it be able to rebuild?

Rebuild what? Will anyone again choose to work in a skyscraper? Which insurance company will cover a landmark tower? Indeed, were the twin 110-storey towers to be rebuilt they would stand like pyramids, colossal empty tombs, in memoriam to a lost civilization. Two months on from September 11, smoke was still billowing up out of the ground, out of the five-storey pit, as if the fires of hell once ignited might never be extinguished. Air thick with powdered asbestos was the enduring lethal residue of terrorism. One-hundred-and-ten storeys had been compacted to one hundred feet of rubble, each storey thus reduced to one vertical foot. By the end of the excavation, the human count was two thousand people lost without any fragment or trace of their material beings.

And if the age of the skyscraper is over, so is that of New York. Nothing big is safe any more. Icarus never flew twice.

What is there to tame the fear, the insecurity? A child in remote Brisbane, Australia, scrawls a message of sympathy to send to New York, but he asks his teacher to leave off his name — 'So they can't come and get me.' While it is his parents' fears that he innocently articulates, they are the fears of an entire culture. This is a culture that has lost the rock on which its ancestors stood, the rock that would not move under its feet when the heavens thundered. What has been exposed is chatter about who I am, why I am here, and what happens to me at death — the mumblings of a secular humanist age, which have been shown up for what they are, illusions masquerading as truth. They are no more secure than those 110-storey towers demolished by disciplined men not paralysed by the thought of death.

Children are more sane. The boy in Brisbane builds his sandcastle with great patience and care, then gains an even greater pleasure from jumping on it, stomping it back to nothingness. His imagination is full of things going up, then coming down, from Jack and Jill going up the hill to Humpty Dumpty's great fall and that of

London Bridge ... except when it comes to his own home and parents. If in the collapse of the towers he had seen his father — the one person who masters the big, threatening, adult world for him — come crashing down and, with him, all protective authority, what could be more dreadful?

Security in the vertical anchors a culture. Thus when Jesus, in the week of his death, withers an innocent fig tree, it symbolises the laying flat of the world, as a wasteland of blackened stumps, so that the Cross may rise. Thus when we are struck by shame, the holy emotion, we instinctively bow our heads and lower our eyes before the imagined sacred power. It is above and about. If the vertical spine of our culture is manifest in the skyscraper, and that is all there is, then we have been pitched into our living wasteland. Usama bin Laden will put it so: my God, Allah, has 'elevated the skies without pillars.'

No one in his or her own individual self has changed. Rather it is the externals that have been shaken, sending shock waves into inner regions in which demons — long kept in check and denied, like mad hounds locked in a dungeon — have started to howl. And some of them have broken free. They are bounding through the deeper passages of the self. No wonder that, up on the surface, things are sombre and lethargic, not as buoyant as usual.

Consider the symbolism! How did our television represent evil, the force that had done this? Having panned around haphazardly for the first two weeks after day zero, drenching its world audience in pictures, it finally focussed, finding itself inwardly compelled by one starkly plain image. The unconscious cue to which it responded reveals much of the inner story.

It had all been brought about by one man, alone on horseback, riding through the wastes of Afghanistan, stealing America's own myth, its hero, its projection of valour. He is tall and handsome, with clear skin and full lips, sun tempered, looking the West and all its might nonchalantly, with a mocking smile, straight in the eye. He wears a fine, longish black beard streaked with grey, a cross between desert nomad and Confucian scholar, yet his bearing is elegant. And it is Satanic. An aura of invincibility radiates from his singular being: sure, calm, decisive, impossible to rattle. He is all of Lone Ranger, Shane, and the man with no name. So big is he that the Western security agencies throw all they have in intelligence and public relations at blaming him, singly, for the entire conspiracy. In their own diminutive being they project the subtext that he is so smart and powerful it must be him.

More precisely, Usama bin Laden echoes the evil character portrayed by America's peerless storyteller, John Ford, in *The Man Who Shot Liberty Valance* (1962), his deeply pessimistic final film western, renouncing the myth of his country and its founding hero. Ford had come to see his own nation's epic story as a failure— and his Wild West is the entire modern secular West.

The first Liberty Valance had valour built into his surname—a reference to the fact that he, in his monumental badness, forced anyone who crossed his path to prove what they were made of: 'What kind of man are you, Dude?' Reborn forty years on, as an Arab, he is no longer simply a frontier thug. This is the bad man with brains. He triggers America's High Noon, and that of all the rest of us around the globe who were baptised in the temple of the West.

One of Usama's charges against America is that it has no courage. Where are its warriors? It thinks it can wage war from behind a bureaucrat general's desk in the Pentagon, fight by long-range missile so its soldiers are saved from danger. On the rare occasion that troops are sent in—Lebanon in 1984 and Somalia in 1993—they are withdrawn at the first sign of blood. 'What kind of man are you, Dude?'

The West has been caught asleep on duty by the revolutionary new phenomenon of mastermind terrorism. It has long been accustomed to the mode of the IRA bomber, just as likely to blow himself up. This time, however, we have been outsmarted in our own domain of strength—functional rationality. A capacity for brilliant long-range planning, mobilising technical expertise, carried out by clear-minded and self-disciplined individuals, has been the key to our civilization. Yet which of our institutions could match the successful hijacking, in unison, of four passenger jets, flown skilfully, three of them proceeding to hit their targets — given the potential for the unforeseen in such an intricate mission, carried out in secrecy without a trial-run under tremendous pressure?

Usama is Satanic. That is, he draws on sacred forces for evil ends. It is as if he knows this. His own crafty manipulation of symbols includes posters depicting him as a saint riding on a white horse (the Prophet Mohammed had also fought on a white horse). The clerical aura that Usama gains from being photographed wearing a plain white turban combines with unblinking callousness. For instance, he boasts on a 2001 al-Qaeda recruitment videotape about the bombing of the warship USS *Cole* the year before: 'The heads of unbelievers flew in all directions, and their limbs were scattered.'

Yet Usama's face speaks of great sadness. This makes him difficult to place: his persona is not simply Hitlerian, a human contagion to be exterminated, after which all will be well. Nor is his role principally that of saviour of his own people. Unlike his forefather, Ayatollah Khomeini, he will not rebuild Islamic societies. He has rather arrived as *our* nemesis. He calls the West a snake, with the United States its head. It is as if the Shane who rode away into the far yonder after restoring order has just reappeared over the near hills, trotting resolutely back on his white horse targetting the frontier town, the hero now metamorphosed into an incarnation of Satan.

Moreover, this defender of the Muslim faith did not

attack the West's religious institutions — the Vatican, Westminster Abbey, or an American synagogue. He rather borrowed the West's own 'power elite' analysis, his list of targets straight out of a radical Marxist handbook. He succeeded in hitting centres of financial and military power. His third target was almost certainly the centre of political power: the White House or the United States Congress.

Usama released a pre-recorded video speech the moment America launched its first retaliatory strike, against Afghanistan. This speech — in its precision of rhetoric, its poetic mobilisation of theological and moral phraseology, the subtle force of imagery — strikes at the nerve centre of the West like nothing since its own Martin Luther nailed the Roman papacy to a Wittenberg church door in 1517, and marked the turn away from the squalor and stagnation of the European Middle Ages. The modern reformer from outside, with slow and measured enunciation, preaches against 'debauchery' and 'injustice':

I bear witness that there is no god but Allah and that Mohammed is his messenger. There is America, hit by God in one of its softest spots. Its greatest buildings were destroyed, thank God for that. There is America, full of fear from its north to its south, from its west to its east. Thank God for that ...

These events have split the world into two camps — the camp of belief and the camp of unbelief ...

To America I say only a few words to it and its
people. I swear by God, who has elevated the skies
without pillars, neither America nor the people who
live in it will dream of security before we live it in
Palestine, and not before the infidel armies leave the
land of Mohammed, peace be upon him.

In September 2001 this man was opposed by a slow,
corpulent bureaucracy named the United States
Department of Defense. It could not even defend its
own headquarters in Washington, with 55
minutes' warning from the first plane crashing into the
New York towers, an hour-and-a-half after the first
hijacking, and knowledge that other hijacked
passenger planes were in the air.

It is as if the man who shot the first Liberty Valance,
John Wayne, had crossed to the other side and was targeting the vitals of the brontosaurus — a creature so
mentally and neurologically deficient that a message
would take five minutes to be transmitted from its tail
to its brain, by which time it was dead. Has the huge
Pentagon building with all of its occupants — the
intelligence centre of Western military might — been
exposed as one of the dinosaurs of our time? This was
a time, we may now suspect, that took to *Jurassic Park*
and its tale of extinct monsters in hideous fascination
with itself: transfixed by what was about to be exposed,
and fearing what, in its complacent corpulence, it had
unwittingly turned into.

The Pentagon is under the Liberty Valance challenge, to prove that it can base an effective war strategy upon its supreme arsenal of aircraft, missiles, and precision bombs. One of Usama's lieutenants will assert: 'Never underestimate your enemy. Military man is stupid man.' Usama himself had brazenly mocked, in a video released two months before September 11 that anticipated the attack:

> With small capabilities, and with our faith, we can defeat the greatest military power of modern times. America is much weaker than it appears.

Consider the symbolism! On the one side there is the American president. Most of the Western world is fearful of the answer that impending events will provide to the question of whether he is the man for the hour. And there has not been such an hour since the Second World War, six decades ago. Jesus often recorded in response to danger: 'My hour has not yet come.' For George Bush junior, it has come. So fate decreed; and meanwhile Apollo sits in judgment over leadership in the West.

Consider the symbolism! Nine days into the new and unmapped order the president makes his address to his nation, and to the world, beamed live via television. It is delivered on Capitol Hill, a name resonant with the grandeur of ancient Rome, the site from where the largest empire yet known ruled for five hundred years. The scene is set inside the House of Congress: it is a stirring speech at length, written by others, delivered to congressmen and senators, to invited members of the American political and administrative elites.

There is some eloquence, with timed, deliberate pauses — at most of which the president receives a rapturous ovation. America is desperate to believe in its man for the hour. He is somewhat wooden, yes, but is this the boyish president who cannot put two words together without sounding like the primary school dunce?

How does he do it? Television shows him addressing this large assembly of the men and women who lead America in a vast, open chamber with no screen in front of him. Nor does he glance down to the lectern to read pages that may be placed there. The truth is that he faces a sheet of glass, invisible from the outside but reflective on the inside so that he can read at eye level, word for word, a teleprompted text projected from the floor. It may well cue pause, pace, and stress. Commentators rhapsodise over his Churchillian eloquence. But Churchill wrote his own great rallying wartime speeches, rehearsed them, and then delivered them off the cuff to his nation and the democratic world. They rang true, and instilled confidence in a people during their darkest hour.

On the one side is this image of the leader of the Western world like a bewildered schoolboy, wide-eyed in his lack of comprehension, shadowed by his advisors to minimize the gaffes — advisors urged on him by his father, in another humiliating signal of no confidence. On the other side, the television screens show the lone Arab on horseback living by his wits, moving invisibly from cave stronghold to secret camp through the Afghan wastes and into the north-west frontier of Pakistan, or wherever he may be. Usama's two leisure activities are horse-riding and reading — his reading, Islamic thought and current affairs. Wherever he has travelled in the past, his large personal library has gone with him.

All this the stunned world observes. It is an instant lesson in culture, a study in the ways and beliefs of the West, and whether it is up to defending its institutions. Swarthy, dark, mature bearded men in white turbans and long, white, comprehensive robes, ruthless fanatics, some of them Islamic scholars, in targeting the West are challenging: You, you prove yourself. Let us see what you are made of. What kind of man are you, Dude?

2 EXCESS

The ancient Greek word was *sophrosune*. Of the four cardinal virtues, it was the one favoured by Apollo. It is the virtue of *nothing in excess*, of moderation — that is, measure or balance. Its literal translation into English is 'saving mind' or 'sound mind'.

Transgressively out of balance, the modern West is measured by the law it violates, by *sophrosune*.

We are the biggest, richest, most powerful civilization in human history. Two centuries ago the Industrial Revolution, pioneered in England, sunk a shaft into a hidden and hitherto untapped source of energy. Fuel would gush forth with such ceaseless profusion as to allow us to conquer the entire world. Suddenly we humans could harness the forces of nature to our ends, developing levels of scientific and technical knowledge to transform what we mined and grew into steel, plastic, and a myriad other compounds, inventing countless new wonders including antibiotics, the jumbo jet, and the microchip. Four of the five age-old physical necessities that had caged the lives of our ancestors in toil and misery were mastered — brute labour, poverty, famine and, in the main, disease. Only war remained.

However, the magic well could not be capped. The geyser of production could not even be controlled. Eighty years ago, the great sociologist Max Weber speculated that capitalist progress would continue unabated till the earth's supply of oil ran dry — a prophecy that was telling, but probably underestimated our technical inventiveness. During the Cold War some feared thermo-nuclear war would bring an end.

By the close of the century it was clear that industrial expansion could not continue as it had. Otherwise, the resources of the earth would be exhausted — the seas fished out, the land over-farmed, rendered barren by overuse of fertilizer and pesticide. The earth's atmosphere was probably warming; human population growth threatened its own catastrophic multiplication, in poverty-stricken areas which could least sustain it; and an excessive use of antibiotics threatened their efficacy, opening the possibility once again of pandemics decimating human populations.

Homer records that after the Trojan War Apollo organised a nine-day flood, to wash away a wall the Greeks had built to protect their ships. It was impudence for those humans to presume they had powers over nature: who did they think they were? We in the modern West have abused our duty of care to the earth

on which we are born, and to the weaker creatures that
share it. As honoured guests at this bountiful feast we
have gorged the food, got drunk on the wine, and
fouled the white linen. Now the god of measure, who
appears with the dawn, has intervened.

Our form of governance, democracy, developed into
an ideal of rule by representatives of the people in the
service of the people. There were periods — notably
the 1950s, and throughout most Western countries —
in which this translated into worthy practice, of a reasonable standard of living, not too much inequality,
and a collective ethos of inclusiveness towards almost
all. In recent decades democracy itself tipped out of
balance. Comment is superfluous when a chief executive of a major corporation is rewarded by bonuses in
the order of $10 million for a year in which he sacks
half his staff. He might be receiving on top of his
bonuses a standard salary of $30 million per annum —
sums beyond the imaginings of ordinary people, such
as an American waitress toiling for $6 an hour.

Likewise, early in 2002 the world's largest corporate collapse — Enron — highlighted the depth of
endemic corruption in the American political system.
A range of committees was set up to investigate the
crash. Of the 248 senators and congressmen serving on
these committees 212 had received donations from
either Enron or its accountants, Arthur Andersen —
also under the same investigation for malpractice.

Tom Wolfe, in his 1987 best-seller, titled this

explosion of excess *The Bonfire of the Vanities*. He focussed on the share and bond markets in New York, the new world of trillions of dollars being speculated daily via computer screens—the very business that was transacted in the World Trade Center. Five years later, the English weekly *The Economist* produced a supplement on finance in which the West's leading experts concluded that the international system was now so huge and complex that no one understood its dynamics.

The terrorists understand it well enough, though. It has been surmised from the levels of unusual trading in futures in the few days before September 11 that their networks made in the order of hundreds of millions of dollars, using 'put options' in markets in different Western countries. Knowing that airline and insurance stock would plummet in value, they cashed in the difference between the old 'sell' price and the post-crash 'buy' figure. This time it is no medieval barbarian who storms the citadel of the West. In fact, al-Qaeda has a business and finance committee, comprising bankers, accountants, and financiers managing its assets across four continents—a network more sophisticated than any previously encountered by Western intelligence agencies.

What typifies our civilization today? Not the cathedral or the Bach cantata; not the council chamber or the court; not the spring festival or the Saturday market. This is rather a culture that has managed to remain standing by encapsulating itself in the package tour through life. So we have immunised ourselves against the demons, and the fear of death. Who may claim to be different from those English-speaking tourists trudging around the ruins of the ancient Capitol on a hot Roman afternoon, filming meaningless lumps of dusty old stone, with no knowledge of what happened on this site that might lift the imagination above its petty anxieties about being fleeced, inedible foreign food, missing the bus back to the hotel, and sore feet?

Meanwhile, at home we speed along super-highways bypassing stagnant hamlets and country towns that might prove disagreeable to the tired gaze of the pampered metropolitan. So it is that many kids who grow up in cities today believe tomatoes are grown in supermarkets.

And what of the makers of our high culture—the philosophers, writers, artists, and composers—those whose duty it is to help their fellow citizens understand their condition, make sense of the lives and times into which they have been cast, help them with their trials? For more than a century the dominant style has been 'modernist', renamed 'post-modernist', projecting the view that life is absurd, that there are neither absolute truths nor moral laws—in short, that nothing is real.

The modern university has betrayed its mission, as have the mainstream arts. To teach that Mickey Mouse is as valuable as Shakespeare, or that a urinal is as beautiful as a Raphael Madonna, or that the seduction of children is not categorically evil, but a mode of self-realization, is to corrupt the most precious of all human resources — the young. Western high culture has operated free from any reality principle. That is, it did until September 11, 2001. The disintegration of skyscrapers is real, even to intellectuals. Mind, vestiges of the old frivolity endured, as in the comment of the modernist German composer, Stockhausen, that this image of destruction was the greatest modern work of art.

The Twin Towers were beautiful. Stately, tall, with a sheer vertical precision, their poised, austere rectilinear forms extruded upwards, and ever upwards, shining blue-silver on a clear day like a Titan's upturned tuning-fork. They were singular — signature to a singular metropolis. A symbol of the heights reached by industrial civilization, they presided over its achievement. One could have dreamed them, when approaching New York by plane or boat from certain angles, or by camera, as a metaphysical gateway.

This was a beauty, however, that came with a cultural warning. It stood in negation to the great Gothic cathedrals of France, led by Amiens and Bourges. With them, the outside is a visual muddle, a dissonance of pillars, struts, and flying buttresses, its single function being to support a structure concentrated on inner beauty. The medieval architects and builders were so little interested in the outer that they did not bother, usually, to complete the cathedral towers, leaving them stunted, like lightning-decapitated trees. Their intention was to create a sacred space of such perfect form that once penitents had left the outdoor light and entered through the portals, and had adjusted to the dimness, their spirits would soar aloft, orchestrated by flutings of vertical stone, illuminated by stained glass. For the best part of a millennium now, it has been inside these sublime, vast chambers that countless humans have sensed themselves carried aloft into the presence of God.

The World Trade Center followed another ancient architectural tradition in the West, one mocked by St Matthew in the metaphor of the 'whited sepulchre', which is beautiful on the outside. The modern resurgence of design that is aggressively indifferent to interior spaces in which humans might feel at home began in Germany in the 1920s, with the Bauhaus movement. Modernist architects instigated the dominant twentieth-century trend towards rationalised, hard-edged, machine-model buildings, using steel, concrete slabs, and plate glass as their favoured materials. From apartment block to skyscraper, the Bauhaus aesthetic produced spaces in which ordinary humans were condemned to live and work in sullen unease.

Here was another manifestation of the self-important modern artist. Building taller, harder, colder was a projection of his own state of being. Contemptuous of those whom he should have been serving, the poor victims who had to live their lives within his spaces, his single aim seemed to be self-promotion. His building shouted: Look at me, how unique, how *avant garde*, how great I am!

The 1989 film *Dead Poets' Society* retold the same story in different clothing, this time with a charismatic poetry teacher exhorting his boys to be like him — creative, sensitive, self-made, contemptuous of all traditions and morals, always ready to 'seize the day', to break bounds. The sub-text prowling under a sparkling surface-narrative of initiation from boy into man is that this prophet of rampant narcissism, this artistic face of modern Western excess, doubles as the prince of darkness. Initiation backfires: the leading disciple fails to grow up. Without any defence against the hounds, he kills himself. Stockhausen walks in the same shoes when he celebrates September 11 as the greatest contemporary work of art — his jaded palate titillated by the fusion of outward beauty with cataclysmic destruction.

By the time the World Trade Center was built, opening in the early 1970s, the impersonality, sterility, and claustrophobia of the concrete box had, at least in its high corporate modes, been softened by plush fittings and spectacular views from window rooms. Executives must have felt more comfortable, yet what they experienced was no more than a polished veneer that was unable to change the basic reality. The skyscraper is unnatural as a site in which humans might dwell at their ease. How could it be otherwise when the population of a medium-size town is crammed inside a vertical post, hermetically sealed, dependent on air-conditioning and gravity-defying, high-speed lifts? Those who relinquish the liberty of opening a window to let in fresh air where they work all day, every day, five days a week, are inviting distress.

The Twin Towers' interior spaces had their own strange ambience. There dwelt a dark crowdedness, especially in and around the lifts: a feel of pressing confinement, of walls too close, of ceilings too low.

Clarity can sometimes emerge from a parallel reference. In the highest towers of the culture of the West, the music of Johann Sebastian Bach is a formidable example of balance, of the integration of inner and outer, in counterpoint to the World Trade Center. Bach is the antithesis to his fellow German composer, Stockhausen.

Of peculiar relevance to our metaphysical crisis today is Cantata 82—*Ich Habe Genug*. Both the words and the tune are telling. Sung low and sadly by a solo male voice to simple oboe and organ accompaniment, its lead phrase translates literally: 'I have enough!' A ripe fullness to the plaintive cry suggests that the words be read firstly as an acknowledgment that my life has been rich. This merges into a sense that I have had my fill, carried by a world-weary gratitude for having been given enough and now being complete—my cup is full, with cup meaning character, experience, and fate. But there is also a third, and darker, undercurrent to the cantata, suggestive of 'I have had enough.' Life has equally been an ordeal loaded with despair, and I am tired of it.

One of the messages out of the wounded pain of this song is that life is serious. Here is a lesson in striving to find the right orientation to the essence of being. Nothing is to be taken casually or frivolously in what we are given. Moreover, any inclination to protest or lament indicates discord. The focus of the cantata — how to orient oneself to one's own death — underscores the responsibility we bear for the entire cast of our earthly span.

The music somehow meditates on the nature of being — who I am, what I have been — in order to possess it in the dark hour. It seeks to find a way of letting the spirit, now grave with finality, embrace the whole. A haunting chant steeped in pity, it is the soul crying out, struggling in its melancholy to contain a life in its entirety, express it, bring it to a fitting completion. It picks up an echo, too, out of the deep, heaving ocean of existence, a companion voice as if from the other side, of the shade-to-be calling out for imminent union.

When Usama bin Laden charges that his war is against 'the camp of unbelief', he targets an imbalance in this life, a restlessness and cowardice unleashed by fear of death. One dimension of the September 11 reality check is for us to rediscover a right relationship to death. In a culture of excess the serious is denied. We have been casual with what we were given, off-hand with what we should be doing with our lives. When everyone chatters 'Me-me-me', 'Give me more', the anchoring truth is: 'I have enough.'

Where are our deep meditations on what we have received, our acceptance of it as generous — we who live in extraordinarily abundant times and places? Where is our gratitude? Where are our wise consolations for the ways in which life has seemed unfair? What do we possess that will carry us beyond the narrow confines of our own egos, connecting us with a grander harmony beyond? September 11 halts us in mid-stride. Listening to Bach should make us ashamed of what we have become.

One of our civilization's tactics in not hearing has been to addict itself to knowledge — the wrong knowledge. To hold the hand of science when the lightning strikes will not bring succour.

It was decided in New York after September 11 that every lump of concrete, every twisted steel girder, indeed every fragment of matter from the Twin Towers would be taken to a special site and tested scientifically. The FBI set to work sifting the debris for evidence. The reality was 200,000 tons of steel, 425,000 cubic yards of concrete — 100,000 dump-trucks' worth of rubble.

This was a self-inflicted labour of such astronomical proportions as only children can imagine — cued from Grimms' *Fairy Tales*. What was expected? The identity papers of a hijacker, probably false? Telltale DNA? Again, the reality principle had absented itself. This was not even proverbial needle-in-a-haystack stuff, given that the burning jet-fuel had cremated everything in the vicinity of where the planes struck, to be dumped in the forthcoming days as ash and dust over Manhattan. New York would breathe in its own sadness.

One aspect of the rubble-sifting was a search for fragments of human remains, which were then DNA tested to match samples from missing victims. It is beyond imagining what such a forensic focus — given the gruesome and usually microscopic relics that were actually turned up — might mean to grieving family and friends.

In May 2002 a new frenzy in search of knowledge flared up, as if on cue timed to coincide with the last rubble being removed from the Twin Towers' site. It appeared that intelligence had been available before September 11 warning of a hijacked-plane assault on American buildings. Both the CIA and the FBI were put under the microscope to examine whether the attack might have been averted. This time, the culture's hyperactive faith in knowledge was on the edge of orchestrating a witch-hunt in search of those who were to blame, for neglecting vital information. It is, of course, easy to be wise after the event. The reality is that intelligence agencies are deluged every day by hundreds of snippets of rumour, opinion, and fact — and mixes of all three.

There was a telling criticism, however, which became public soon after September 11: if the CIA had had agents on the ground in Afghanistan the plot might have been exposed. Lifestyle comforts in modern America had made it unacceptable to demand that agents learn very difficult languages to levels of fluency before being dispatched to alien and dangerous places to live by their wits in Spartan isolation and privation. The CIA had become dependent for information on an armoury of hi-tech gadgets — listening-in devices, unmanned spy planes, and surveillance satellites. It had mountains of knowledge, all of which turned out to be useless. 'What kind of man are you, Dude?'

The media feeds the inability to sit still with its own endemic lack of restraint, blasting forth incoherent facts and images — its grains of knowledge whipping up a sandstorm. What has happened to our sense of respect when we can tolerate television reshowing a video sequence of people falling to their deaths from the towers? These images were even used to advertise the station's next news broadcast. They were finally pulled off the air, at least indicating some remaining tissue of shame running through an indecorous culture.

Rushing around after billions of fragments of evidence, propelled into a futility of frenzy, it was all driven by the anxiety to know. If only we had the right knowledge, we might understand. But understand what? Why it had happened ... what had happened ... where we have gone astray ... the roots of our unease? We are even unsure about what has been broken, let alone about how to put Humpty Dumpty back together again.

This is a civilization that has lost contact with the saving truth. On September 11 it was found out.

3 THE BLUEPRINT

So what is going on? Is there the hand of a big story behind the scenes shaping the surface events? September 11 was not the beginning; far from it. It belongs to a precise and detailed narrative that in its modern Western form has been scripted for over a century, its story line fixed and immovable, coercive, retold again and again in order to break through a fateful impasse. Every time so far, the ending has proved unsatisfactory — an exit into chaos. 'Narrative' should not mislead, send the false signal that what we are dealing with here is fiction, a figment of the imagination, not real. Indeed September 11 may turn out to have been the climax.

We, like the preceding four generations of our Western ancestors, have been living out *Heart of Darkness*, Joseph Conrad's nasty little tale from 1899. This squalid three-act farce held the entire twentieth century in thrall, to be retold again and again, both in lived events and in fiction that stencilled reality to its

form. To know where we are today we need to retrace
the path that led to the doors of the World Trade Center
in New York on September 11, 2001.

Act One is the point of departure. The scene is the
absurd city. For Conrad's central character, Marlow, it
is London, and Brussels. In fact, it is every modern
Western metropolis — any German, Italian, or
Australian who stands back today and thinks this problem is exclusive to America needs to think again.
Marlow puts it this way:

> I found myself back in the sepulchral city resenting
> the sight of people hurrying through the streets to
> filch a little money from each other, to devour their
> infamous cookery, to gulp their unwholesome beer, to
> dream their insignificant and silly dreams.

Order is maintained by holy terror of a triple
constraint: scandal, the police, and the lunatic asylum.
Also there is the comfort of a fixed address and a
butcher on the next corner. Once you awaken to the
absurdity of such a life — beautiful on the outside,
dead within — you are compelled to flee. Marlow
chooses to journey inwards via outwards, to the heart
of Africa, for adventure beyond the confines of civilization, up a river into the barbaric wilderness — in
order to get the blood flowing, in order to live.

Most Westerners who try such a route merely take
their absurdity with them. Marlow observes a French

warship off the West African coast, firing canon arbitrarily into the jungle. A century on, American president Bill Clinton, the first to go after Usama, will dispatch *Tomahawk* cruise missiles into near-empty Afghan caves, and bomb a Sudanese aspirin factory under the delusion that its product is nerve gas. Marlow scorns such mindless representatives of Western civilization as 'reckless without hardihood, greedy without audacity, and cruel without courage.' The main effect of the Clinton raids was to turn Usama into a hero throughout the Islamic world.

Act Two is the journey. This is *the* journey — single, definitive, inescapable — of the modern West. All denizens make it, although their travel is usually both unconscious and unwilling. The journey begins historically, with the event that set its formative imprint on the twentieth century — the 1914-1918 World War. The cultural elites on both sides argued zealously in favour of going to war. They imagined a means of escape from the absurd city. It would provide them with something to believe in — Nation — and an adventure to purge the lethargy that had set in after what they saw as decades of comfortable bourgeois mediocrity, a darkness in which they might be able to come out a bit, and prove themselves. But Nation is an ideal with no metaphysical depth; violence is not therapeutic.

The reality was four years of shelling the fields and towns of Flanders and Northern France into oblivion, the slaughter of an entire generation of European men.

In what would become the most influential poem of the century, T. S. Eliot projected the devastation as metaphor for the state of Western civilization. *The Waste Land* (1925) in its first draft had as its epigraph the climax from *Heart of Darkness* — the answer to the question of what we are here for, the ultimate meaning of human life: 'The horror! The horror!'

Even more extreme attempts to find something to believe in through politics followed. Hitler offered Germans a cause to inspire and direct their lives. Communism attracted disenchanted Europeans with dreams of a redemptive social order. The reality on both fronts was another heart of doom, even darker than what had come before.

A new generation in the 1960s woke up one day to look out the window, and saw their own cities as absurd. They were alert to the excess that surrounded them, and inclined to action, at least to finding a way of proving themselves, charting a different path, one out of the metaphysical slum into which they felt they had been born.

Once more they took to politics in search of a saving belief — this time a brand of anarcho-pacifism. True to the coercive script, blind to the trap, they were, like Marlow, seduced by the intoxicating beat from the jungle, but plotted their course through music and drugs. Demonstrating against their own era's war — Vietnam — made their practical politics. This was journey by negation, the repressive constraints of a run-down civilization to be stripped off, allowing regression into the child idyll of a love-and-play utopia set in perpetual springtime.

In the absurd city it is impossible for boys to mature. For women, with their different resources, the path is more obscure, a story remaining to be told. At issue is initiation, the rite of passage which every vital human society takes as necessary for growing its boys up to become men. Male initiation centres on an ordeal conducted by the elders, directed at killing off the boy-self. This is to free the youth from dependency on women, and especially mothers — successful initiation cuts the psychic umbilical cord. A second function is the reining-in of the anarchic playfulness of childhood; the development of inner controls without which post-puberty hormones are likely to explode into delinquent violence.

Marlow is typical of the modern Western male in that he has to design and perform his own initiation. It turns into an act of self-mutilation, for Marlow receives no help. There are no elders to guide his passage, to restrain him when he strays too close to danger, to welcome and celebrate him at the end. One of the effects of September 11 is to have put the male elders who run America on a near-permanent television show, responding to events, spelling out strategy. The most boyish-looking president in living memory, George Bush junior, leads them. Is there not a message here?

When Marlow reaches his heart of darkness he is

confronted by a human skull stuck on a pole, looking straight at him. He finds himself staring into the mirror. It is the same for all those boys who do not undergo the initiatory passage through symbolic death, the extinction of the child self — taking place during a long and terrifying journey through the underworld. They are left stranded with the shades. No one has led them back up into the world of the living. These cultural orphans have been abandoned in the nether world, a 'no-man's land' in-between the territory of the living and that of the dead. They are condemned to a state of demi-life — dry of energy or direction. Their capacity to move paralysed, it is little wonder that depression and youth suicide have risen steeply in many modern consumer societies.

The West's archetypal tale of the journey to the land of the dead suggests that growing up is no easier for women. It is Eurydice, the young bride, just married, who is left stranded in Hades. Her husband, Orpheus, fails in his task of leading her back to new life — as an adult woman. In this story the man himself chooses not to grow up, being more in love with his music than with his adoring bride. His weak desire closes off the possibility of female fulfilment. In his nervous evasiveness towards women, Orpheus may be taken to represent the whole culture.

Meanwhile, an entire century during which the West's industrial power and wealth multiplied, without check, was being shadowed by retelling upon retelling of the original *Heart of Darkness*. After *The Waste Land* came, to list some of the more prominent, *Waiting for Godot*, *The Third Man*, *Apocalypse Now*, *Blade Runner*, and *Dead Poets' Society*. However, the most fateful of all appeared in 1999: the film *Fight Club*. Its story ends with American skyscrapers being blown up, the modern metropolis disintegrating in terror.

This prophetic, ugly film opens with a vicious caricature of the contemporary city, Conrad brought up to date. The central character, Jack, suffers from chronic insomnia, permanently dazed by tiredness — 'nothing is real, only a copy of a copy of a copy.' His job takes him to horror accidents, to calculate statistics for a car manufacturer to determine whether defective models should be recalled. His one pride and joy is his apartment, and its fashion furniture that he has bought off the *Ikea* catalogue. His spotlessly clean refrigerator contains condiment jars but no food. His one relaxing activity is visiting therapy groups, night after night, pretending that he belongs, for instance, to a company of men with testicular cancer. Then it begins.

First, let us return to the Conrad blueprint. Act Three is the meeting. The journey into the heart of darkness is to search for the man who has already gone there, travelled up the river, and discovered the saving truth. The mythic source for the story is the episode in the Life of Jesus on the Road to Emmaus — when two wayfarers, on their journey of journeys, are joined by a stranger whom they only come to recognise hours later over supper. On the instant He disappears.

Marlow travels in search of a new Christ, the one for our time who might point the way, teach how to live, explain the meaning of it all. His name is Kurtz. However, Kurtz has failed. The modern knight of faith has tried everything, lived life to the full — as journalist, orator, musician, painter, explorer, idealist, conqueror, accumulator of wealth, lover of women, teacher of disciples. His life principle has been to seize the day, in order to know the truth. Yet he has found nothing in which to believe.

Marlow meets a soul gone mad, one who has surrendered to the savagery of a human life beyond any limits. He has kicked the world to pieces. Left with nothing above or below him, nothing to obey, Kurtz has given himself over to an orgy of rampaging bestiality — his life is one of pure excess, without check. His house is surrounded by skulls on poles, all but one facing inwards — the exception stares Marlow and, with him, the rest of the modern West straight in the eye. It challenges: Are you actually alive?

Fight Club Jack in his own waking sleep meets his Kurtz, who promptly blows up the *Ikea* apartment. So much for the absurd city! Today's charismatic leader targets men with no opportunity for valour. His solution to their testicular problems is to set up underground clubs in which they meet at night to beat each other to a pulp. Violence charges the testosterone, restoring vitality — men discover a spring in their step, a pride in their maleness. A blood brotherhood is forged, a movement born.

The fight clubs attempt initiation. However, the final stage of the ritual is left out—the rebirth of boys as responsible adults. The initiates are left stranded in perpetual youth. Men today—perhaps it has always been the case—are clever at devising strategies for not growing up which they stubbornly, tenaciously defend. The *Fight Club* mode is the male horde. In the wider society, teenage boys take to such groups in their myriad forms, ranging from the loose collection of peers gathering in a shopping mall to the sports team and the gang. These groups teeter on the edge of brutishness. Boy-men huddle within the secure confines of collective power and name, bonded by the rhetoric of blood brothers and mates, and shared mob rage, clinging together in order to hide their brittle individual identities.

Failure in the film story is due to the leader not having found the saving truth, so he has nowhere to lead his reborn emasculates. He is just another Kurtz, empty of belief, stranded in his own heart of darkness. The West continues along, making no progress in its metaphysical condition. The failed saviour of 1999, like his predecessors, creates a fascist militia from his devotees. Its goal is inevitable, by default—to counter self-pampering greed with a bacchanalia of gratuitous destruction. His ultimate target is American skyscrapers which house finance institutions: the story ends with him blowing them up.

There is no saviour today. Does this mean there can be no leader? John Ford, when he made the film *Young Mr Lincoln* (1939), his study of America's pre-eminent hero president, projected a humble lawyer, youthfully gawky, a man of the ordinary people. Ford knows that the rite of passage from child to man is the key, so it is the initiation story that he tells. His Lincoln has to triumph over the male horde. Ford asks the deep question: from where does he get the inner force and the lonely fortitude? Youthful Abe, in need of sacred authority, of powers from beyond, is pictured riding a mule, Jesus-like, a black silhouette in a tall top hat. This Lincoln also gains strength from praying at the grave of his fiancée, and talking to her apparition. Communing with the dead, in the particular form of his companion spirit, a female one, gives him fibre not contained within his own character and its instinctual resources. The film ends with his entry into manhood —which means acceptance of his vocation, and the tragic shape it will bestow on both his own life and that of his country. Ford's Abraham Lincoln is the saviour as leader.

Marlow's crisis comes when he realises that there is no saviour—that his hoped-for Jesus, his Kurtz, whose name means 'short', is withered and prostrate, a man hollow to the core. The dying Kurtz is just a voice, whispering: 'The horror! The horror!' Marlow himself falls sick and almost dies. He has seen that he is utterly alone.

The one non-illusory thing that Marlow has found is his vocation—as a ship's captain. He discovers that he is good at getting a ramshackle steamer up the treacherous River Congo into darkest Africa and back to the coast. This is his first appointment, giving him a job to do, one that keeps his mind from straying too far into wild imaginings. Through his journey into the jungle, and back, he finds that he can steer. He has discovered something modest in which to believe and, with it, a sense of responsibility—caring for the well-being of his crew. He has happened upon the Lincoln transition. But does he make it himself?

In the modern West, *vocation* has been the best bet. Each particular one, whether it is waitress or gardener, accountant or architect, mother or carpenter, comes under its own law—the law that governs its order of right conduct. When the fork is crookedly placed, the pruning clumsy, the figures sketchy, the building at odds, the attention elsewhere, or the door jams, a law has been broken. The job has not been done justice. What this means is that everybody who enters through the gate of vocation leaves the lawlessness of their own egos behind. Whether they know it or not, at that instant they come under an obligation to something bigger than themselves. Finding a central life-activity, no matter what, to which they are able to devote themselves, body and mind, heart and soul, commits them to seriousness. Taken out of the flimsy cocoon of individual being, now on higher duty, they are freed, even if only temporarily, from the absurdity and the horror.

The gift to Marlow on his initiation journey is that of vocation. By giving him something to do, it keeps him moving. It keeps him sane. Of this he is obscurely aware, in the needling, worried reflections that accompany him throughout his voyage—as he steers the ship of his fate. Nevertheless he cannot free himself from the illusion that his journey's purpose is to meet the one who has found the saving truth. He remains, in his own psyche, dependent on another, not having it in him yet to be his own man.

Marlow is again representative of the modern West, this time in being mistaken about the nature of what he is doing, about where he is going, even about whom he seeks. From the particular to the general, he is modern everyman, and every woman.

In New York, Marlow was the firefighter. After the terrorist attack, when the need to find heroes became paramount, the men of the New York Fire Department took centre stage.

The firemen were called to duty once the planes struck the towers. They did what they were trained to do: strive to extinguish the fires and rescue those trapped. On arrival at the site they entered the buildings, both still standing, and began to climb the stairs. Of all the poignant reports of the morning of September 11 that were to be published in the following months —and there were hundreds in *The New York Times* alone—none would equal one that was repeated again and again by those who managed to escape. As they were descending from impending death, racing towards safety against a time-clock without knowing when zero would strike, or even if it would strike, rushing down flight after flight of narrow, congested stairs, they were passed by firemen trudging the other way, carting their heavy gear, their grim faces looking upwards.

Of the 340 firemen who would never re-emerge, ordinary men doing their duty, how many would have been able to suppress their own dreadful thoughts, hoping against hope that their tower would not collapse on top of them? If a sense of vocation is to command the times, surely it must speak in the hardest, most hopeless and, thereby, most valiant circumstances?

These anonymous heroes caught America's attention. The rest of the Western world looked on, too, in hushed, aghast pity at their courage. Their self-sacrifice was quite alien to the surrounding culture and its ways—even unnatural, embarrassing, to it. Their example put the issue of courage in the floodlights, evoking the unconscious response in almost every observer: 'No, I would not have been able to do that!' With a rapt, nervous focus on the firemen, there followed the second chain of inner questions—concerning how, why, and what it might signify. Did their sacrifice somehow give meaning to it all?

In the blueprint, vocation on its own is not enough. Once Marlow returns to London he finds himself back in the same old absurd city. He shows no inclination to seek another commission. The drive, the passion, or whatever it is that might be needed to live, is not there. While another ship would allow him to keep moving, actually and symbolically, his solitary voyage has proved so overwhelming, so debilitating, that he has lost the desire to captain again. His being is stranded up the Congo with memories of Kurtz, haunted by the horror of the skull. His last remaining enthusiasm is to tell the story.

A failed initiation shadows the life, and leaves nothing. Commitment to an ethic of vocation, which may have once been kindled, flickers then goes out. The light of revelation has not shone. Boys are left homeless, with no future. Will the surviving firefighters find more to hold on to, or will they, like Marlow, be left stranded, in their case in the ruins of the Twin Towers?

Usama bin Laden is different from the *Fight Club* Antichrist only in coming from outside, entering as the unwelcome stranger. He, too, is possessed by a mania for destruction—the base motive driving his life. In a 1999 television interview, Usama even used the phrase 'heart of darkness' in describing America's Somalia disaster.

Yet his presence is ambiguous, and very difficult to digest. He is Kurtz masked by an aura that is alien while, at the same time, familiar. His smile is Satanic, while seductively mysterious. His Semitic features, his free, long, black hair, and his doleful expression, awaken in many a Western psyche its own iconic memory of the Jesus face. In how many American churches does a similar-looking visage fill a stained-glass window or a spotlit sacred niche? The Antichrist comes with confronting, nightmare familiarity. This time the command is not that of Jesus: 'Courage! *I am*. Don't fear!' but Kurtz's: 'The horror! The horror!'

There are two Books for this man who travels with his own large personal library. There is the holy book, the Koran. And there is al-Qaeda's own *Encyclopaedia of the Afghan Jihad* — 7,000 pages, written over five years from 1989, a training manual for guerrilla warfare and terrorism. Its first ten volumes cover tactics, security, and intelligence. It is based on experience drawn from fighting the Soviets in Afghanistan, as well as from culled United States' and British military manuals, and diverse technical sources. One volume, for example, catalogues with forensic detail and precision the different characteristics of explosives.

Again the West has been pillaged. The founders of the eighteenth-century French Enlightenment produced the world's first encyclopaedia in homage to education, knowledge, and progress. For over two hundred years, the *Encyclopaedia Britannica* extended this civilized tradition, making available useful knowledge to everybody who could read. Now a man driven to kick the world to pieces has adapted one of Western humanism's finest creations into an instrument of

Satan. He rides with the Koran in one saddlebag, and eleven volumes on the mechanics of mass murder in the other.

America now insists on standardising the spelling of his first name as 'Osama'—spooked by the word's opening three letters. The transliteration into English commonly employed before September 11 was 'Usama', accurately reproducing the Arabic pronunciation. As its nemesis, he is shadow other of the West, an insider—*USA* plus a hummable lilt. Usama is the demonic creation of the West: his conception is old; his gestation, long; his birth, late; and his manifestation, a mockingly contemporary and particular USA guise.

4 THE HOLE

The hour appears to have coincided with flagrantly weak political leadership. It is as if the fates have decreed that the way through this will not be directed by presidents or prime ministers. To know the script would paralyse them. It follows that those who hold office are not to blame. They exist rather as reflections of their societies and their discord—papier-mâché dolls.

With September 11, 2001, the denizens of the modern West have entered a new era. The cue is *Heart of Darkness*, supplying the form but not the ending. Events so far suggest that we are in store for a long narrative, broken up into distinct phases, each with its own logic. The year 2002 inaugurated Chapter Three.

Chapter One ran from September 11 to October 7, the day America began bombing Afghanistan.

During those first four weeks the Western ego was at its most exposed—open and transparent—before its defences regrouped, using tactics of denial and avoidance to take up positions modified to counter the new fears. Like Humpty Dumpty, it had taken a great fall. Even before September 11, it was so brittle that to intrude on its domain was to step on eggshell. The slightest insensitive step, and another fragment would be crushed.

This is the boy looking out through the man's eyes, the boy who never managed to grow up—for his culture had neglected to initiate him into manhood. His hurt ego swings between extremes, from a cowering whimper to foot-stomping rage. There is no dignity in an adult given to tantrums. There is no balance. On the one hand, he studies every fragment of rubble from the ruins, feeling compelled to rush around before it is too late to gather the tiny pieces, and to start gluing them back together, one by one.

On the other hand, the blood rushing to his head, he chafes at the bit to start bombing. That ego, fearful without form, prays that all the president's warplanes and all the president's forces can put Humpty together again. Once its forces are marshalled, its might unleashed, the single super-power shall obliterate the enemy. The Western ego, unnerved by disorder, cannot bear things out of place.

We are a good-hearted people, asserted the president, and we are strong. We will destroy Afghanistan, in order to rebuild it anew. So ran the glazed fantasy, the unnerved displacement—for the unconfessed dream here is to restore America, restore the West, and thereby restore the *Ikea* apartment. Then everything will be back in order, as it was.

The first American title for its mission, *Operation Infinite Justice*, signalled the extent of derangement during the opening phase. The emblem of justice is the scales, weighing carefully one side against the other. Its logic is that of balance; its mood, cool sobriety; and its reach, rigorously finite. Yet the disturbance to our equanimity is without limit, starting with testicular fears. Is our culture and its institutions in a shambles? Can we regain control? Or will we be paralysed? The hounds stir in the deep passages of the self.

A sign of how poorly the West was digesting its new condition occurred in the eighth week. The heroes of September 11, the men of the New York Fire Department, refused to leave the Twin Towers' site because the remains of 230 of their comrades were still interred there. Some of them took to punching the police who were trying to remove them — the very police who had been the other servants of the public conspicuous for their courage on the day of terror. New York's Mayor Giuliani, the one man after the strike to have displayed leadership qualities, himself became unhinged, threatening to throw the firefighters in jail. Here was an early sign of the great calm and care that will be needed for restoration. If these courageous men are frozen in their mourning, unable to let go, it is because they have not been guided adequately.

After the initial shock, the fear was that of

bereavement. The entire West had been turned on the spot that is the present — forced to face backwards, to question what had been lost. Except this time, apart from family, friends, and fellow workers of the three thousand victims, no one had the least idea of what was gone. An ear-shrieking bell, a fire alarm rousing the modern West from its slumber, had sounded. The alarm stirred the fear, too, of what was still to come.

It was during these early weeks that the first faint flickering of a new nightmare appeared. Let us call it *the hole*. It would spread as time passed. The blueprint story had been wrenched sideways and forced into a tight new form that made it much more difficult to wear. Marlow, on awakening to the absurdity of city life as he knew it, had been able to venture on his own long, slow journey, allowing him to adapt to the heart of darkness stage by stage, as the full horror that awaited him around the next bend in the snake river progressively came into view. He had time to steel himself, to prepare himself, for the skull on the pole guarding his saviour's house — the skull awaiting him, Marlow, and him alone, challenging: 'Are you actually alive?'

On September 11 there was no time. One moment it was 8:45 on a glorious late-summer, early-autumn morning in New York, an average Tuesday, with normal people going about their daily affairs. By 10:30 two hijacked passenger jets had been speared into two towers, and both those 110-storey skyscrapers had collapsed. The descent into the horror had been instantaneous by the big-story clock which governs these things. During the abstracted, slow-motion, shock consciousness of those 102 minutes, CNN's television commentators were representative of the human reaction, merely able to fill the silence with aimless, semi-coherent talk. They were caught off guard when, virtually on the stroke of ten o'clock, the first cloud of debris rose—the signal that Tower Two, the south one, was imploding. It seemed an age before they understood what was happening before their eyes.

Suddenly, ruins were all that was left—although, as a word, 'ruins' seems quite inadequate. And physical excrescences gushed forth, the tangible, breathable projections of the psychic trauma: smoke, fire, dust; more buildings collapsing, this time smaller ones; then more smoke and dust.

From that time, what has held everyone's attention, mesmerising the West, not just those in New York, has been the Twin Tower wreck—the site. That a third plane had been crashed into the Pentagon building was quickly forgotten. They called it Ground Zero, oddly choosing the military term for the land area directly under a nuclear explosion—which, at Hiroshima, had been triggered in mid-air, to flatten the city while reducing fall-out. Here also was an oblique reference to 1792, the year that the French revolutionaries had calibrated as zero after abolishing the old calendar: history would begin again from that year, that day, they declared.

The hole, sixteen acres broad, was filled with 100 vertical feet of rubble, most of it below ground level. Jagged sections of stressed steel-lattice and concrete rose like grisly skeletal arms disgorged by an earthquake, or teetered like the stern section of the *Titanic* groping upwards to stay afloat as she was dragged remorselessly down, slipping silently into the hole, icy and silent as an open tomb — which is what it was. Left precariously erect were repeating sections of closely spaced steel perimeter-columns, which in the ground floors were thicker and set wider apart before they curved together in pairs as they ascended, to mimic Gothic arches. They now evoked the ghostly ruins of a gigantic cathedral — such as Beauvais, which had risen too high for its buttressing, and collapsed — or a medieval monastery that had been vandalised and abandoned after King Henry VIII's land grab.

Smoke would keep rising. Two months on, whenever a crane removed a hefty piece of steel, flames would roar out of the pit. It was as if an entrance to an underworld had been uncovered, one smouldering red with anger at the disturbance. It was being excavated, not by high priests attuned to potential sacrilege, in rightful fear of where they trod and what they touched. Nor was it their secular descendants, the knowledge devotees — archaeologists — at work. The employees of Bovis Lend Lease, an Australian construction company, beavered away on site around the clock, and finished the job in

May, three months ahead of schedule—in a fury of efficiency.

Those men and women working in the hole, construction workers employed in deconstruction, would end up reluctant to leave, just like the firemen felt before them. As the job advanced they would confess to dreading its completion. What would they do next? Where would they go? Or, as one of them put it, who would they be?

For the thousands of artisans in the mid-thirteenth century who travelled from all across France to Chartres to build the great cathedral, it would presumably have been difficult to return home, back to erecting stone cottages. The wreck of the Twin Towers generated kindred enchantment—by negation. On that earlier occasion, a long time ago, the labour had been offered devoutly to inspire a tower rising to God. Today it cleaned out the ruins of a temple dedicated to finance. In either case, people were at work within a sacred site.

The hole had become the centre of belonging. Under floodlights at night, this was a blazing hubbub of activity, of industrial civilization showing its muscle: the cranes; the bulldozers; the front-end loaders; the laden dump trucks struggling in low gear up the ramp, their engines screaming in high revs; and swarms of workers in their helmets, heavy jackets, and breathing equipment. The object of a systematic frenzy of clean-up, the site looked like an in-between world, a space-age purgatory in which, if you carried out the right tasks, you might be released, upwards. To be busy was to be 'all right'. Once the Herculean labour was complete, so ran an obscure fantasy at this stage in the life of the hole, a door would be revealed—and it might open.

But why the rush? The frenetic deconstruction in the hole was like a gothic replay, a drama cast with giants, of surgeons with high-precision equipment in a modern operating theatre—cheerless, tragic theatre. Yet surgeons do have to work against the clock in order to save the patient. Here the sedated body was the cultural corpus of the West. There was no hurry.

On the contrary, to get it wrong would merely lead back into the absurdity. A man down a deep hole with a shovel and no way out, dazed by panic, starts to dig. Dirt flying up all around distracts him from the fact he is digging himself further in.

Joseph Conrad makes it clear that there are two quite different orders of absurdity, which should not be confused. They were in New York. Once routine, everyday life in the modern city (the absurdity which Marlow and *Fight Club* Jack flee) is transformed into its polar opposite—the horror—the logic changes.

Early in his journey, Marlow comes across an accountant working in a company station up the river. He is surrounded by chaos: rusting machinery, abandoned, wantonly smashed building materials, and rotting corpses. Nothing works. Marlow has entered hell

on earth. Yet the accountant is impeccably dressed in
the sweltering tropical heat—high starched collar and
tie, white cuffs, alpaca jacket, varnished boots—and
is holding a green-lined parasol. His office is orderly;
his books, immaculately correct. He is absurd, yet in
the midst of nightmarish social disintegration his care
for outer forms creates an oasis of calm, endowing him
with a certain dignity.

On September 11, the veteran American war corre-
spondent Scott Anderson happened to be in
Manhattan. He reported in *Esquire* magazine coming
upon a crowd in front of the Supreme Court building.
In order to donate blood, groups of people were being
corralled into pens defined by yellow police tape.
Their blood type was marked in big black letters on
their arms or sleeves. One man was shouting hoarsely:
'O-negatives, we urgently need O-negatives.' However,
there was no one there to take blood, nor any vehicles
to take people to where it might be given. Anderson
concluded that this was organisation for organisation's
sake, the invention of a plan of action as security
against the anarchy, and the first step in rebuilding an
orderly society. It was both absurd and inspiring.

The absurd here is subordinate to a form—just as
the accountant serves his vocation, his pride as a man
refusing to bend. Marlow admires his backbone: 'this
man had verily accomplished something.' Similarly,
the little boy takes satisfaction in his sandcastle before
stomping it flat. We might term this middle-rank

absurdity. It has little to do with metaphysical emptiness. Indeed it may indicate the opposite.

Once the hole was empty, what then? Had the rush been driven by the illusion that a completed job would muzzle the hounds? Or by a belief in the dated cliché: cleanliness is next to godliness? This might translate as: to clean up the mess is to restore order, a restoration attracting the saving divinity. Once there was order in the darkness, there might be light.

Alistair Cooke, in his weekly international radio report, *Letter from America*, has observed that Americans are prone to interpreting everything in life as a 'problem'. Other Westerners are less susceptible to this habit of mind. The advantage of deeming something a problem is that, by implication, it is a condition that can be fixed. Here is another symptom of the addiction to knowledge as tranquillizer. Whatever the hole had become, it was not a *problem*.

The firefighters had refused to leave the site where their comrades had fallen. The instinct of the living was that the dead had not been properly laid to rest. The unrecovered physical remains, while hopelessly lost, endured as a presence. The entire spirit of this place was one of distress and disturbance. An ancient tradition in the culture of the West leads us to mark a headstone with the words 'Rest In Peace', and to feel that *RIP*, the initials that represent these three words, reflect the truth. It is the duty of the living to honour *RIP*. The firefighters, on edge, bewildered, somehow felt responsible for setting things right. But their job was fighting fires and rescuing survivors, not spiritual restoration.

Construction workers, with no practical reason of their own, became fazed by a similar spell. Or was it charm, or charisma, or anti-charisma — like anti-matter? The hole had become its own centripetal field of force, a seductive vortex sucking attention towards it. Correspondingly, everything beyond its perimeter had been rendered inert.

What would be left once the hole was clean? The relics were being rapidly removed, to a 53-year-old landfill on Staten Island with the macabre name of 'Fresh Kills'. When they were all gone, where would the firemen go? Would the construction workers be able to move on? Perhaps hope, too, had been trucked to Fresh Kills — for DNA testing?

What if it was merely a hole — no exit door, just the crushing weight of the fallen spirits that echoed across its emptiness? Its elemental reality was as a cemetery — a cemetery that had been bulldozed then systematically cleansed. It would stay a burial ground of uneasy sorts for those thousands who had lost, without any physical trace, the ones they loved. For them it threatened to remain a spirit graveyard — eternally unredeemed.

The hole spread. It was there inside an olive-green US mail pavement post-box, which in the days after September 11 was plastered with notices and appeals, and photographs of missing people, with the phone numbers of parents, husbands, and wives, lovers, friends, work-mates, and employers. Had anyone seen the missing? Perhaps a miracle would happen. Perhaps these notes would turn into letters and fly in through the imaginary slot, to be collected by the uniformed post-man, or a guardian angel, and be delivered to the miss-ing. The post-box would stay, for most, a black hole.

The relics to appear at Fresh Kills Landfill includ-ed fragments from *The Three Shades*, a bronze sculp-ture by Auguste Rodin: two headless male bodies, life-size, and a severed foot had inexplicably survived. Along with two other Rodins, they had been the show-piece of the bond-trading firm Cantor Fitzgerald, where they had been displayed in its head-office lobby on the 105th floor of the north tower. The company had occupied five upper floors in this building, where one thousand employees had worked. Of these, two-thirds had perished in the attack. In the north tower, no one had escaped above where the plane struck — the stair-wells down had been blocked, and organizing the unlocking of the door to the roof was botched, in spite of an hour-and-a-half's grace.

Rodin had worked for decades on *The Gates of Hell*, drawing his inspiration from Dante's epic vision of the underworld. *The Three Shades* formed one piece in the ambitious whole, positioned on top of the outer frame of the gates, with *The Thinker* directly under them, dominating the entrance itself. Cantor Fitzgerald also owned a miniature cast of this famous image of brooding thought, using it as its company symbol. The bond-trading executives would have assumed that they could separate the single piece from the setting intended by the sculptor. It was, nevertheless, brazenly far-fetched to link a renowned homage to thinking, unique in the culture of the West, to plotting world finance-indicators and dealing in bonds. The donor, company co-founder B. Gerald Cantor, once owner of the world's largest private Rodin collection, would have known the original intention behind the works.

Before September 11, the corporate audacity could be shrugged off. But when the object of the *Thinker's* troubled concentration — and thereby that of the multitudes who have identified with him — is the hopelessly dark state of his own soul, what then? Any attempt at precise allegory here is foolish, and presumptuous. Yet the association is grim, and hard to dismiss as coincidence. Dante's original three shades had been in life, in the main, good men, admirable elders of ancient Florence — punished for sodomy.

The hole was there in the amnesia. The steady clearing of the site in the nine months between September and the following May seemed to advance in exact counter-point to a descent into forgetting, as if with each loaded dump truck going up the exit ramp another psychic step was taken downwards. The ancient Greeks had warned of oblivion. They deemed it the natural human state — out of weakness, the human impulse is towards forgetfulness, to daydream on and on through life. *Truth* equates with *not-oblivion*, the moment when the mists shrouding the river Lethe —which contains the waters of forgetfulness—lift, permitting clear vision. As the hole emptied, the realm of oblivion spread, like a winter-swollen lake.

The second metaphysical tower of the West, Apollo's other injunction, directs: 'Know thyself!' The Delphic authority singled out for special censure the delusion that, in order to live, it is better not to know. And it specified the type of knowledge involved. Oedipus became great amongst humans because of the wrong knowledge—he was smart at answering riddles, and at performing his duties as king. But he was blind to his own horror nature, to the fact that it was his father whom he had killed, and his mother whom he had married. Along the road leading away from Delphi through the plains of oblivion—for our Greek ancestors, if not for Dante and our Roman Catholic Christian ones—lie the gates to the underworld.

The hole grew, too, in the absence of any plausible idea of what to do with the sixteen-acre site. There were those who suggested that the Twin Towers, or a diminutive version of them, could be rebuilt —as if what had just happened were some commonplace city demolition, this hole a waste of fabulously valuable real estate, and it was time to move on. Others wanted a simulation in laser lights. A memorial park might work, or perhaps a commemorative sculpture?

There are precedents in the modern West for

unspeakable coldness in this realm. Today, visitors to the tastefully restored German city of Munich will likely travel on the sleekly clean and efficient underground rail system. They will read on the standard route maps adorning every station that one line has its terminus at Dachau. What was once a key Nazi concentration camp, one known for its extreme brutality even in that infamous company, has been turned into an outer suburb, with new housing estates where contemporary people live everyday lives. Shakespeare questioned: 'What's in a name?' We might ask: 'What's in a place?'

The enormity of September 11 was turning into bewilderment and denial. The pride of Western civilization had taken a body blow, with the two sublimely grand towers gracing its most cosmopolitan city, the emblem of its industrial and technological prowess, having been reduced to a hole. It is impossible to chart the extent of the deflation, the degree to which the cultural ego is now in withdrawal, cowed and whimpering. One sign is the reach and depth of the vast emptiness that has taken over from the trinity of monuments— the Statue of Liberty, the Empire State Building, and the Twin Towers—that once symbolised New York and America.

The moment calls for an artist in the highest traditions of the culture of the West—an Old Master, one of the stature of Bach—who interprets the times to itself, in a work that is both beautiful and true. To redeem the

hole, and everything it contained, would require grav-
itas and pity, sorrow and prayer, gratitude and wonder
—a creation that was of the hole, yet rose out of it,
reaching beyond it.

Are three thousand shades owner-occupants? If so,
they stand proxy for the West. Many, we can assume,
are unsettled. There has been no fitting *RIP*.
Meanwhile, the fear among the living is of *not-being*:
no revelation, no conclusion, just back to the absurd,
waiting for nothing to happen. Imagine in a year's time,
when visitors come—from wherever in the West—to
view the site of the World Trade Center in New York,
and look across and down. If their honest response is
'It's just a hole!', Kurtz has once again prevailed. The
modern pilgrim might as well have exclaimed: 'The
horror. The horror!'

5 SUCCESS

Chapter Two opened on October 7, 2001 when the United States began its war against Afghanistan. *Jurassic Park* struck back The next three months would prove to be the period of high success and the restoration of morale. This was charted by a steady recovery in the stock market — by Christmas, Wall Street had returned to its September 11-eve levels.

The main phase of the American war in Afghanistan would last a mere ten weeks. The first month, entailing precision bombing over terrain with little vegetation, demoralised the enemy troops, who had no air defences. In the north they had dug in, but their trenches merely served to delineate their positions. Air power on its own, guided by British and American special forces on the ground, precipitated the first retreat. Northern Alliance forces — a coalition of different Afghan tribes and interests — then swept the country from north to south, encountering minimal resistance.

On November 9 the Taliban regime that had shel-
tered Usama bin Laden still controlled 90 per cent of
Afghanistan. Ten days later it was a mere 15 per cent.
By Christmas the assault was over, a victory smooth,
swift, and almost comprehensive, with negligible
American casualties—fewer than twenty deaths. This
was a result that the military strategists had not
dreamed possible. English defence historian John
Keegan summed up the Taliban:

> Visually and rhetorically impressive though they
> were, they were probably never the force they
> appeared to Western observers. They had made
> themselves hated by ordinary Afghans, who adhere
> to a comparatively moderate and tolerant form of
> Islam. Many Taliban fighters, moreover, though eth-
> nically Pathan, were not the fierce Afghan mountain
> warriors of Kipling's ballads but town dwellers from
> Pakistan. Poorly trained and badly equipped they
> lacked the quality to conduct protracted operations
> in a modern war.

The American air strikes were prudent and
restrained. A new order of Western rationality—smart
bombs—ensured that civilian casualties were
relatively low, as was the wider destruction of neigh-
bourhoods and towns. Targets were methodically
demolished, and over several raids, often building-
by-building and vehicle-by-vehicle. The Afghan

official in charge of repairing Kabul airport marvelled:

> I have been through the Russians. I have seen
> Hekmatyar in action and the Northern Alliance. This
> is just incredible. The Americans seem to have been
> 98 per cent accurate.

In the weeks following September 11, many in the West predicted that an American attack on Afghanistan would trigger the uprising of radical Islamist groups and mob riots throughout the Muslim world—in Saudi Arabia, Egypt, Pakistan, Turkey, and Indonesia, just to name the leading potential centres of unrest. In part, this was a reasonable reading of volatile polities. In part, the old appeasement sentiment had resurfaced: be nice to your enemy, and he will leave you alone.

From his speeches, it is clear that Usama anticipated the same. One of his aims was to provoke, through an American over-reaction to terrorism, just such a fundamentalist revolution throughout what he termed *Islam Nation*. He seems to have a special affinity with a paranoid strand in European Marxist-Leninism, which held that the worse you make things, the better they become, even among your own people. The assumption was that once conditions are forced to one extreme, with maximum destruction and mayhem, people would rise up, ushering in the opposite extreme. Usama thus conjoined fanatical religious Puritanism with a radical brand of early-twentieth-century secular materialism.

It did not turn out that way. For once, Usama was wrong. In the first week after the air strikes began there were nine major anti-American demonstrations in the Middle East. A month later, as Taliban resistance began to collapse, there were none. The streets of the Muslim world fell silent. As usual throughout history, the successful deployment of power had proven persuasive. America had taken charge; its overwhelming superiority of firepower, intelligence, and elite forces decisively answering: 'What kind of man are you, Dude?' President Bush was himself beginning to grow into his office, at times almost looking and sounding authoritative.

And yet, was this victory more than one battle in a long war? True, Afghan territory would no longer provide the key location for the training of Islamic terrorists. Peter Bergen estimates that in the year 2000 there were around a dozen training camps operating there — his book, *Holy War Inc.* (2001) was the pre-eminent source on al-Qaeda before Rohan Gunaratna published *Inside Al Qaeda* in June 2002. The closing down of these camps was a result that on its own vindicated American action.

The Afghan aftermath, however, may prove less smooth. If the Americans remain, they could well find themselves subject to protracted guerrilla combat. The Taliban and al-Qaeda forces that survived the war have merged into one unit dedicated to fighting the invaders —on territory that is ideally suited to hit-and-run raids. Usama has long wanted to draw American troops into just such a situation, where his patience and his focus on preserving the strength of his forces would likely prove a major long-term advantage. If American forces leave, Afghanistan could easily revert to an anarchic free-for-all between warring tribes and factions, opening itself up once again as a safe base for Islamic extremists.

The attack on Afghanistan was successful in terms of closing down the headquarters of global terrorism. There were other gains. By Gunaratna's count, al-Qaeda lost sixteen of its 25 top leaders, including Muhammad Atef, its chief military commander and brother-in-law of Usama (although there was no independent verification, and his death is disputed by some European intelligence services), and its director of external operations, Abu Zubayday, who was captured in Pakistan three months later. Yet the war had failed in its principal aim. Usama bin Laden had escaped. His main Afghan base, a vast cave complex in the Tora Bora mountains between Jalalabad and the Pakistan border, had been bombed, then assaulted by ground troops. It was thoroughly searched and occupied. But the occupation had been too slow. The quarry had flown. The mastermind lived on.

This is a campaign in which the capture or killing of Usama, and his deputy, Ayman al-Zawahiri, is almost certain to cripple al-Qaeda as an agent of mega-terrorism. The modern Western corporation is not useful as an analogy here. It is readily able to grow another head, with one chief executive replaceable by an equal. Al-Qaeda is more like the German Nazi government during the Second World War: the assassination of Hitler would have broken it. But that was not so easy to carry out.

6 THE LONG HAUL

It was now the year 2002. In this unfolding story of
indefinite length, Chapter Three slowly dawned. After
the preceding day of triumph, spirits were high. Now
the skies turned sober, layered in greys, their striations
wispy, elusive. 'Red sky in the morning, shepherds'
warning.' This day was shaping up as the test.
Overnight, the degree of difficulty had soared. To start
with, it was quite unclear what to do.

Yet something had to be done. If momentum
faltered the fear would return—the practical fear of
the next terrorist attack, and the deeper fear. The
strategic objective was clear-cut: to carry on in pursuit
of Usama's al-Qaeda organisation, capture or kill its
top leadership, destroy its training camps, and thereby
deter the Islamic states that had been covertly
sponsoring terrorism—notably Iran, Iraq, Syria,
Pakistan, Sudan, Somalia, and Yemen. In addition,
America's dignity as the global super-power, and with
it Western prestige, depended on its effective

continuing prosecution of the anti-terrorist campaign.

Otherwise, America would soon be mocked for choosing the Taliban regime in Afghanistan as its target—a bunch of ill-equipped amateur fanatics with negligible public support tyrannising a country with a feudal political structure as stable as quicksand. What about the powerful centralised states that had been backing Islamic terrorist organisations for decades?

America proclaimed that Iraq was the leading candidate in this category, its despotic leader Saddam Hussein having survived the 1990-91 Gulf War—prosecuted by president George Bush senior. American pride decreed that it had unfinished business in Iraq. Moreover, Saddam appeared to have gained in power, shrugging off attempts to curtail his development of weapons of mass destruction.

Yet it was Iran that had played the more significant role during the period that Usama bin Laden was based in Sudan, between 1991 and 1996. One of Usama's achievements had been to forge links between the Sunni and Shiite branches of Islam in the interests of world terrorism. He united the world's two most dangerous terrorist groups, al-Qaeda and the Lebanon-based Hezbollah, which Iran backed. Between 1996 and 1998 some 10 per cent of Usama's outgoing phone calls from Afghanistan went to Iran, an indication of the enduring relationship.

Even so, links to sponsoring states are tenuous, and have declined since the end of the Cold War. A feature of Usama terrorism is that it is globalised, his own wealth and organisational abilities meaning that he has not been dependent on any of the oil-rich states for backing. His financial mainstays from outside the organisation tend to be wealthy Arabs, many of them respected individuals from Saudi Arabia, Kuwait, Qatar, and the United Arab Emirates.

At this level, the West is again chasing a shadow of itself. The al-Qaeda leadership is full of technocrats — setting the style for the September 11 hijackers, who were indistinguishable in look from young American businessmen. Usama himself has a degree from Jeddah's King Abdul-Aziz University in economics and management. His top aide, Deputy Emir General, Egyptian Ayman al-Zawahiri, is a physician, while other principals have degrees in engineering, accountancy, psychology, and computing. Peter Bergen likens al-Qaeda to a multinational holding company — one of Usama's aliases is 'the Director'. Bergen's other allusion is to Usama as the 'Pied Piper of holy war'.

Rohan Gunaratna dubs al-Qaeda a 'virtual' organisation, because of the seemingly wraithlike structure whereby it is built from cells or clusters that know nothing about each other. It is a horizontal network with regional command nodes — for example, operations in the Balkans were at one stage coordinated from Turkey. Its preferred means of communication, especially since 1998 when Usama realised his satellite phone was being monitored, is the human courier.

The successful reversion to such a pre-modern mode of communication as the courier highlights Western dependency on the wrong knowledge. The CIA, for all of its multi-billion dollar funding and thousands of employees, is a bureaucracy lacking the only effective counter—men on the ground. Here, its technological surveillance is next to useless.

The Director has installed a thorough planning system, based on painstaking preparation. The first of three stages in designing an operation is advance surveillance by intelligence teams so that the attack body can rehearse the action within a training camp, often with the aid of models of the buildings or vessels targeted. Al-Qaeda has developed its own intelligence wing, reported to be of a strength comparable with Western government agencies. Second, a support group goes to the target area to arrange safe-houses and vehicles, and to move in weapons and explosives. Third, the operatives arrive.

Even Western cosmopolitan technocrats depend on cultural authorities, if unwittingly—first and foremost, Adam Smith, the secular prophet of the free market, and Thomas Jefferson, the prophet of the democratic-humanist pursuit of happiness. With the new terrorism, the 'belief' appears to have come from an older generation.

Mentor to the younger Usama was a Palestinian, Sheikh Dr Abdullah Azzam. Together in 1984 they founded the Afghan Service Bureau, in Peshawar,

Pakistan. Three years later Azzam turned it into al-Qaeda — the first international *jihadist* network. Azzam, born in 1941, had been educated in theology in Damascus before taking a doctorate in Islamic jurisprudence from Cairo's al-Azhar University — the Arab world's pre-eminent tertiary institution. He went on to combine the role of charismatic professor with the practical application of his mantra: *'Jihad* and the rifle alone: no negotiations, no conferences, and no dialogues.' The goal was the restoration of the *Khalifa* — all Muslims around the world united under one ruler.

Al-Qaeda was conceived and designed by Azzam. He wrote its founding charter. Moreover it was he who started the Afghan *jihad*, travelling the world recruiting men and soliciting money. He succeeded in setting up offices in thirty different American cities. Meanwhile, Usama alternated between fighting on the front line against the Soviets and funding and organizing from the base in Pakistan. It is in telling contrast that neither of the two presidents who have opposed him — Clinton and Bush junior — have been to war.

The two Arabs together set up the first terrorist training camp, in Afghanistan's Paktia province on the legendary north-west frontier. Usama would name his eldest son Abdullah.

Azzam was assassinated on November 24, 1989. Although Usama was the designated successor, he had become, in latter years, distant from his mentor, their views increasingly in conflict. Usama's own single-

minded ambition was to dedicate al-Qaeda exclusive-
ly to global terror, a worldwide *jihad* with the aim of
destroying the United States and Israel, and restoring
the Caliphate.

Gunaratna argues that Usama himself sanctioned
the assassination of his own patron, teacher, and guide.
The Egyptian faction of their organisation carried it out
—using a bomb containing 20 kilogrammes of TNT,
activated by remote control. The bomb also killed
Azzam's two sons. Gunaratna writes of Usama's
'exceedingly duplicitous nature':

> By acquiescing in Azzam's murder, Usama freed the
> organisation from being constrained by its founder's
> guiding principles and rules, allowing him to refash-
> ion it in his own image, and channel it in directions
> he preferred. He is not an original thinker but an
> opportunist, who surrounds himself with a good team,
> manages it well but borrows heavily from others.

We might suspect that, given Usama's pre-recorded
'Luther' speech and the range of metaphors he uses
(such as likening the enemy to the head of a snake),
the phrase 'Not an original thinker' underestimates the
presence, imagination, and ingenuity of this man.
Then there is his flair for organisation.

Usama's ally and sponsor during the Sudan period
also warrants attention. Sheikh Hassan Abdallah al-
Turabi was the 60-year-old intellectual grey eminence

guiding the radical Islamist government in Khartoum, its spiritual leader. Turabi, like Usama, was no medieval primitive self-cocooned in archaic Islam. His father had brought him up to love traditional Arabic culture and its poetry, and to develop a scholar's knowledge of the Koran. The father was equally a modernist, sending his son to English-language schools. Receiving Western scholarships, Turabi went on to take a master's degree in law from London University in 1957, followed by a doctorate from the Sorbonne in 1964. He had mastered the elite academic institutions of the West. He also travelled widely through Europe and the United States. He then returned to the Islamic world with an intellectual and tactical framework for assaulting the 'Great Satan'. It was based on: 'Know thine enemy!'

In 1996 Usama moved his operations from the Sudan to Afghanistan, using his family background in major highway and public construction to continue his work from a decade earlier, building vast underground facilities. By the time of September 11, 2001 he had developed al-Qaeda into a multinational terrorist organisation of such reach and prestige throughout the Muslim world that it was regarded as the very highest honour for anyone to become accepted as a full member of it. Recruitment was subjected to rigorous screening, with only a small elite gaining entry. Al-Qaeda had built cells not only in Islamic societies, but in every country that housed Muslim migrant populations of any size — with the open social boundaries and multi-cultural tolerance of the liberal democracies making them particularly vulnerable. Western intelligence puts its strength at anywhere between 10,000 and 110,000 trained members — a wide range indicative of the poor quality of available information, due to the blatant failure of our security services.

The first proven, major terrorist attacks orchestrated by Usama were bombings of the American embassies in Kenya and Tanzania in 1998 on August 7, the bombs going off almost simultaneously. August 7 had been the exact day in 1990 on which the first US troops were dispatched to Saudi Arabia. Usama is fastidious about timing and dates.

He had almost certainly instigated a series of earlier actions, from the 1993 bomb attack on the World Trade Center in New York to the massacre of 58 tourists at Luxor in Egypt in 1997. He may well have been behind the successful bombing of the American military compound near Dhahran in Saudi Arabia in June 1996. Four weeks later, TWA passenger flight 800 crashed off Long Island, killing 230 people.

The crash of TWA800 had wider implications. Although a two-year investigation by the American National Transport Safety Board and the FBI ruled out terrorism as a possible cause, there are grounds for suspicion. The 'mechanical failure' explanation seems to have provoked the terrorists into more extreme acts. Usama made this explicit in a 1996 interview, warning of operations that would have a bigger impact on the enemy—ones the West would be unable to ignore. Such operations would require careful preparation.

After September 11 the United States took to the risky tactic of misinformation. The administration had decided that it was in the national interest to cover up, wherever possible, anything that might corrode public morale. The American media fell dutifully into line. Only those inside know the details, of who rang up whom, and when. It is worth recalling George Orwell's metaphor: there are times in which a climate of opinion is so coercive that the lions jump through the hoops without the tamer having to crack his whip.

Dan Rather, the news anchor for the US television network CBS, a celebrity in his own right, described the pressures to conform as like the threat of 'necklacing' in South Africa. The result, he later lamented, was self-censorship: 'The fear is that you will be necklaced here, you will have the flaming tyre of lack of patriotism put around your neck.'

Let us note three instances in ascending levels of seriousness. In the week following September 11, French television news covering the World Trade Center site reported looting, and that it could only have been carried out by firemen or police. CNN released the same footage, but excluded the looting story—after all, the firemen and the police were the heroes of the hour.

Early in November an Australian journalist wrote a story for the Melbourne *Age*. He had been outside the

United Nations' building in New York when he saw a man of Middle-Eastern appearance leave a large back-pack between two cars. The journalist rang the local police, and within minutes the area was swarming with police, firemen, and bomb-demolition experts. The journalist was surprised that there was no mention of the incident on either the evening television bulletins or in the newspapers the next morning. Puzzled, he rang the same local police station, only to be told that they knew of nothing of any significance having happened the day before.

On November 12, American Airlines flight 587, bound for the Dominican Republic, crashed into homes in New York three minutes after take-off from John F Kennedy airport. Eyewitnesses reported the first sign of trouble as the tail section of the plane having fallen off, followed by one of the engines. Authorities rushed to the media almost instantly to discount terrorism, their first hypothesis being that gross mechanical failure had caused the accident. After a few days their story changed, again with suspicion-inducing, implausible haste: now they speculated that the slipstream of a Japanese airliner had created such turbulence as to shake off the Airbus's tail section.

The National Transportation Safety Board in Washington took over investigations. It has subsequently published a series of updates, the eighth by May 2002 when the chairman announced that the analysis would continue to be long and painstaking.

All its reports so far have been inconclusive, while stressing that there is no indication that the crash was anything but an accident.

The circumstances, however, do point to terrorism: the location (New York); the means (another long-range flight); the date (two months plus one day from September 11); and, above all, the inexplicable disintegration of an aircraft. Also there were similarities to TWA800. Stories circulated within the top level of Western intelligence circles of a missile fired from a yacht. It is understandable that the American government would do what it could to preserve national morale — too much panic might stop people flying, investing, trading, and consuming, perhaps inducing an economic depression with immeasurably dark consequences, including for the war against terrorism. Capitalism depends on confidence. Two nudges in the right quarters would be more than enough.

In February 2002, misinformation turned into disinformation. The Pentagon talked openly about 'black propaganda', the planting of misleading stories in the world's media. It had set up a new department, the 'Office of Strategic Influence', with the Orwellian task of influencing opinion abroad. There was outrage in some sections of the American media. The Pentagon's unselfconscious admission that it would engage in such activity suggested that Washington had come to accept misinformation as normal.

The inference was that government now assumed it

was self-evident that lying and cover-up were permissible in the national interest. It is not surprising, then, that shrewd, well-informed observers of current affairs, in and out of America, ones not normally given to conspiracy theories, should have lost trust in the government and some of its central institutions — notably the CIA, the FBI, and the departments of Defense and State. Scepticism, too, appears justified over reports from the National Transportation Safety Board.

Meanwhile, its European allies were sorely trying the United States — one reason for its clumsy attempts to influence overseas attitudes. There has been significant Western opinion since September 11 levelled against American action in the Middle East. In its most extreme form, it has held that America deserves what it gets for acting as a super-power bully, crudely and recklessly pursuing its self-interest under a hypocritical veneer of altruism; that American capitalism flourishes at the expense of increasingly impoverished masses in most of the rest of the world; and, furthermore, that aggression in Muslim countries will merely provoke more terrorism. The latter claim blames American sanctions during the 1990s for the deaths of hundreds of thousands of innocent Iraqi civilians, mainly children.

The assumption here is that it is abnormal for countries to act out of self-interest. All do, and always have. To criticise a dominant state for using its power is like blaming a lion for roaring. In fact, as a world super-power, America has been as benign as might be realistically expected of it. It does not invade the territory of others, nor enslave alien peoples, nor even set up puppet states. In this it is quite different from its predecessors — from the ancient Romans, Spanish, French, or British in the Western sphere, to the Persians, Moguls, or Turks. Moreover, on occasion, America *has* acted selflessly — as, for instance, with its military intervention in the 1990s in former Yugoslavia, where it had negligible strategic or economic interests at stake.

America was also suffering from traditional European envy, accentuated during phase two by the success of American military might. France, Germany, and the others had been shown up to be separated by an unbridgeable chasm from 'number one', in the stark terms of their capacity to mobilise effective power. Stock allusions to continental Europe's superior civilization — including jokes about the vulgarity of American tourists — began to sound tinny. When the president finally listed Iran as one of the principal backers of terrorism, the Europeans, including Britain, fled for cover. George Bush's term, the 'axis of evil', linking Iran, Iraq, and North Korea, gave them the excuse to tut-tut about extremist language, and to retreat.

Leaving aside the awkward inclusion of North Korea, the simple fact was that the American president was right, and understandably put out by the fickleness of his allies. Just as Europe had dithered about intervening during the 1990s in the disintegration of Yugoslavia, so it was once again starting to behave like a fading dilettante.

Washington was on its own, and frank about its policy options. With the best hi-tech intelligence system in the world, it still could not detect Iraq's stockpiles of chemical and biological weapons, or the underground bunkers in which Scud missiles were stored. Even if the Pentagon were to locate them, could it bomb without causing an environmental catastrophe? At the same time, an invasion of Iraq was to be contemplated only after very careful calculation — for one thing, the Afghan campaign had temporarily depleted the US arsenal of smart bombs and missiles.

There is no evidence to link Iraq to September 11. The secular Saddam Hussein is not a natural ally for al-Qaeda, a body within which religion is the leading requirement for membership. The long haul was becoming ever more fraught with difficulty, both conceptually and practically. The American campaign was at risk of stalling.

An ancillary strategy began: helping governments with Islamist terrorist problems, providing their forces with communications, intelligence, and equipment. Georgia, Indonesia, and Yemen were early candidates for Pentagon assistance. President Bush put it this way: 'So long as there's al-Qaeda anywhere, we will help the host countries root them out and bring them to justice.'

America made another diplomatic move of momentous historical significance. It forged a military, as well as an economic, alliance with its half-century-old super-power enemy. President Bush signed off in May with President Putin of Russia on an arms deal that would scrap three-quarters of either side's nuclear arsenal over the next decade. As well, Russia was invited to non-voting membership of the North Atlantic Treaty Organisation, the military body which had been set up in 1949 with the purpose of defending Western Europe against invasion by the Soviet Union.

The Cold War was truly over, thanks to Usama bin Laden—by the way, something for which he himself claims credit, linking the end of the Soviet Union to its defeat in Afghanistan in the 1980s. The new alliance was crucial, given the geo-political position of Russia, and its ties with Middle-Eastern states such as Iran—to which it has been supplying nuclear materials. The campaign against terrorism is reliant on Russian support.

Besides, Russia was displaying a more clear-sighted reading of Usama than were America's old European allies. If September 11 did not by itself inflict a devastating reality-check on the dilettante position, the all-too-real and continuing terrorist threat that now confronts the West should do so.

There is a *doomsday scenario*. The Western press, while covering elaborately almost every facet of September 11, and its after-effects and potential repercussions, has been strikingly negligent about providing concrete detail in this area. Perhaps it is a case of necklacing. The principal threat is the 'dirty bomb'. Discussion of it will suffice here to make the point, without the additional need to outline scenarios that might follow chemical or biological attacks on major Western cities. The American regime has repeatedly, under questioning, singled it out as the leading danger. President Bush, on first being briefed about it in November 2001, is reported to have lost his temper, and demanded that the government's top priority immediately become the eliminating of any possibility of such an attack.

The dirty bomb is a relatively simple device, consisting of a quantity of conventional high explosive such as Semtex packed with radioactive material. It can be fitted inside a suitcase. The radioactive material might be supplied from spent fuel rods stolen from a nuclear-power installation, or from a canister of plutonium bought on the black market. The Islamist-dominated state security agency in Pakistan has access to nuclear materials. Stories circulate of made-up suitcase bombs being sold by ex-Soviet military personnel. The International Atomic Energy Agency in Vienna has warned that more than one hundred countries inadequately monitor — never mind prevent — the theft of radioactive sources.

The weapon is easy to transport, to almost anywhere without arousing suspicion. From Usama's track record, we should assume that such a bomb would be effectively prepared. The radioactive material, plutonium or whatever is used, needs to be processed in small enough fragments or particles to disperse widely — golf-ball size pieces would be relatively easy to locate with Geiger counters, and clean up. The particles need to be large and heavy enough not to blow away on explosion.

Plutonium is lethal to breathe in, but it needs to be particle-size to be dangerous — and as such is likely to blow away. Otherwise it is, at least in physical if not psychological terms, near harmless. Also, it is hard to obtain. On the other hand, radiation from spent fuel or fission products — which are much easier to obtain — is a lot more dangerous, not needing to enter the human body to prove fatal eventually.

A dirty bomb detonated from the top of a high building in Washington or New York could render the city uninhabitable with radioactive pollution for a decade, a century, possibly forever. In the opinion of Alan Parkinson, an Australian mechanical and nuclear engineer who oversaw much of the cleaning up of the Maralinga atomic-bomb test site in the South Australian desert:

> Whatever the type of radiation, it would be very difficult to achieve a hundred-per cent removal, and I believe removal of all the alpha emitters (plutonium) would be impossible.

Even were a clean-up to be declared effective, who would take the risk of living in a once 'dirty' city?

Usama might follow up such a catastrophe with the demand that America withdraw its forces from everywhere else in the world, starting with the Muslim holy land, Saudi Arabia, followed by the abandonment of Israel. Or else! The president would likely retaliate with his own explosion of military might.

'With small capabilities, and with our faith, we can defeat the greatest military power of modern times.' A second bomb is detonated in another American city — any one, anywhere. At that point, it is all over. (It took two atom bombs in 1945 to force Japan to surrender.) America withdraws into total isolationism, turning itself into a police state, expelling a majority of its own Muslim citizens. World trade comes to a standstill. Every nation is on the instant forced back onto its own resources, in many cases plunged into a Darwinian survival of the fittest. United States-Canada-Mexico, as one bloc, is probably self-sufficient — and the American historical tendency has always been isolationist. The same may prove true for greater Europe. The irony is that the Middle East would be the first global region to descend the African path into poverty, overpopulation, and anarchy. Such is the doomsday scenario.

Which leaves the question of timing. Every month that passes without a major incident occurring helps the West to relax, back home in the *Ikea* apartment.

Forgetting is aided by cover-up. At the same time, the American administration continues to issue regular warnings. In May 2002 its vice-president, Dick Cheney, went so far as to assert that another terrorist assault on America was certain. In a precarious balancing act, the administration urges against complacency whilst spreading misinformation to protect morale.

A growing sense of ease throughout the West, assuming that things are back to normal, bobbles above tremor waves beneath the surface. Three-quarters of New Yorkers continue to believe that there will be another terrorist attack on their city. Children in faraway California continue to have nightmares, in fear of the future. The stock market continues to exhibit the jitters, its rise during phase two followed by sinking over the long haul — due to the tandem threat of terrorism from without and corporate collapse from within. A climate of excess had licensed parallel orders of complacency and corruption.

It is possible that September 11 was singular, not to be repeated. There always remains an off-chance of a single stroke of luck, and that al-Qaeda will melt away as a mega-terrorism danger following Usama being killed or dying from his kidney disease — after all, he has his own renal dialysis machine, with his deputy, al-Zawahiri, acting as his personal doctor. However, it would be lunacy to count on this.

Usama has shown that he works by means of

careful and methodical long-term planning. The Director is part-chess master, part-construction engineer. The first September 11 operative was moved into the United States in 1994, seven years ahead of the attack; the 20 hijackers received eighteen months of intensive training. Usama does not rush. He may strike tomorrow; he may strike in five years' time.

7 ON BEING

The hole was spreading. There was another hole two thousand years ago. Carved into rock in Bethany, near Jerusalem, it was a tomb containing the four-day-old corpse of Lazarus. Jesus shouted into it: 'Lazarus, come forth!' And a figure staggered out of the dark, apparition-like, stinking with decomposition, swathed in white linen, even his face bound in cloth. The sisters of Lazarus, Martha and Mary, were overwhelmed with joy. Jesus' disciples, who looked on, were delighted. This story has continued to speak to the modern West. We all know its outline.

Yet none of those present in Bethany understood Jesus' intent. It was not to show off his magic tricks — he regarded his ability to perform miracles as a low-order power. More seriously, the beloved disciple John, who tells the story, makes clear that its meaning is not to do with compassion for the sick, the dying, or for those who grieve over the dead. Jesus had snorted angrily at Mary who was weeping for her dead brother.

She did not understand. She, whom he loves, should know better. He tells Martha to forget everything she has ever learned, everything she believes about the meaning of life, and death. All she needs to know is that, as he puts it enigmatically: 'I am.' This story is about the nature of *being*.

His teaching is to do with *ego* and with *I*. Mary's weeping had been self-centred — what am I to do now that my brother, whom I loved, is forever gone? Jesus brings Lazarus back to life not out of sympathy for friends in whose Bethany house he has been a regular guest. Whether Lazarus dies yesterday, today, or tomorrow is of little account here. If Jesus grants Lazarus a few more years, so what — indeed, the return to life is satirised, in the form of a comic figure lurching blind out of the rock tomb.

The angry snort, the shout into the hole, and the farcical rebirth shock Mary. She is mystified. His attention has been more on her than on her dead brother, whose plight she, too, has strangely forgotten. Then it happens.

It is in her, she now understands, what she seeks. She had not been drawn to Jesus, as she had previously assumed, by his noble self as master, teacher, and friend. The charisma was rather in the unadorned presence — what he calls the *I am*. It has, on the instant, been transferred back to her. She forgets her own existence, her ego-insecurities and ego-attachments. She fetches the most valuable thing she owns — a jar of

precious oil, worth a year's wages. Lavishing it on
Jesus' feet, she anoints them. She discovers giving for
the simple sake of giving, not in expectation of any
return: right giving. She serves, and through service
expresses her gratitude. The particular act, anointing
the feet, is arbitrary yet complete. It is her sandcastle.
Through her unselfconscious extravagance — which
we might term, right excess — she finds herself. Her
fragrance fills the room.

What Marlow had sought up his river was the
fantasy saviour, the one who would point the way,
instructing him how to live. At the Inner Station, where
Kurtz dwelt, Marlow comes upon a house surrounded
by skulls. We could imagine them as Rodin's shades
locked up in a container at Fresh Kills Landfill.
Marlow had come upon precisely what he sought to
escape, and there the hopeless truth was revealed to
him. He had zeroed in on his own wasteland. The Jesus
who teaches Mary of Bethany directed her to the true
Inner Station.

The music of Bach is, unlike Marlow, in harmony
with the spirit of this Mary. To place oneself in its
vicinity is to be granted a sense of profound order. In
spite of the worst that fate can dish out, in spite of
every capricious turn, it calms the seeming futility, and
cleanses the mess and the waste. Whether outside the
Bethany tomb, or down in the hole, it instils a spirit of
things being all right — *I* am all right. Everything is as
it should be. Everything is in its proper place.

Supreme order fills the emptiness — and, care of this music, it prevails. Bach himself presents a vital engagement with being, with what it is to be human. His musical offering brings wholeness, a completion that invites the listener to join in: 'I have enough!'

So where do we find ourselves today? What is the lesson we have to master for the sake of our wellbeing? The test facing the American regime mirrors the life-challenge facing all occupants of the cultural space that is the modern West. This play of public events is a grand projection of the private wrestling to make sense of the earthly condition. It is thus a double play: one script is focussed on material security; the other, on ease of being. Those concrete, objective external events set in motion by September 11 provide an armature onto which may be flung the tangle of inner desires, anxieties, and hopes that preoccupy us all. From there may come perspective and reconciliation.

At the outset, there is one single, clear, rational strategy. It is to restore order, and by means of decisive action. This is the fairy-tale model, and simple. Once a dragon appears the hero is forced to employ all his guile and skill to kill it. He is rewarded with living happily ever after — end of story. Such is the fantasy, and it remains compelling for adults. Yet it is childish.

When the horror and the absurdity rise to the surface, to confront us with their dispiriting truth, we want an adventure narrative to follow. In the blueprint tale, Conrad's Marlow sets off for darkest Africa. A complete story will give shape to the formlessness of oblivion—at least, that is the hope, even though in Marlow's own case it seems to fail. Thus it is, to choose another illustration, that in the principal area of cultural consolation in the modern West, the television soap opera, the genre of police or detective drama is unmatched for its lasting popularity.

Police shows provide the audience with a formulaic vehicle for immersion in the facts surrounding a case of extreme disorder—crime is against the run of everyday life in the absurd city. And the master writer in the detective genre, its godfather, Raymond Chandler, painted his city, Los Angeles, thick with absurdity—as was the life of his world-weary hero, Philip Marlowe, the explicit heir to the first Marlow.

To arouse sleepy attention from the lounge-room couch, a dimension of horror may be injected. The viewer is drawn along from start to finish by a strong narrative thread. If only real life were like this! Mystery and suspense add spice. Finally comes the climax, followed by the gaoling or killing of the perpetrator of alarm. Order is restored. Life is resolved. The community is revitalised and lives happily ever after.

So we pass the time, superimposing plans and patterns, the sense of project buoying us along. In actuality it may be buying this apartment, getting that job, finding intimacy with this man or that woman, creating a family—or rushing to clear a mountain of debris out of a hole. Snapping at our heels is the *Heart of Darkness* dual menace.

From rear-left comes insomnia, the walking sleep or living death of the absurd city. The firemen who refused to leave the Twin Towers site were sinking back into that abyss.

From rear-right comes insatiability. This is Kurtz, his failure to find fulfilment in achievement feeding a greater restlessness. No project ever satisfies — so there is never the reflective drink in the evening after a full day's work, or happy weariness after a job well done. The symptoms may be more subtle. Perhaps the evening brings a different disquiet, that of slim pick-ings — the sense that I should feel more rewarded than I do. Ill at ease in myself, I should be more grateful for what I have been given. Or the satisfaction is short lived; as with the war in Afghanistan, the pleasure of success quickly gives way to worry about what to do next.

Worst of all, and most common, the slipstream may bring greater turbulence; fear that the tail-plane will fall off. Then follows agitated acceleration into the next project, that it be The One. *Being* is out of balance.

So much in the West today is predicated on the fairy-tale model — the hope in decisive action, followed by success, leading to happiness. Even European envy belongs in this camp. Old world resentment is not against America having chosen the wrong path. After all, each and every Western society is on the same track. The simple need is to be powerful — 'What kind

of man are you, Dude?' Europe wants to be America.
Thwarted, it puts on that facet of the pacifist persona
which psychologists as different as Nietzsche and
Simone Weil have read as merely a cloak for power
envy.

An enduring imbalance in the story is the absence
of women. In *Heart of Darkness* there is no redemptive
female presence. Kurtz has two women, a mistress and
a fiancée, both cardboard silhouettes, like shades flit-
ting harmlessly distant in the background. Marlow is
on his own, without any accompanying warmth or
understanding—one reason why he is profoundly run
down. With September 11, too, all the principals are
men—from Usama to Bush, from secretaries of
Defense and State to other world leaders, from firefighters and police to former mayor Giuliani. The
cultural atmosphere is a one-dimensional male canopy.

This reflects a lack in the modern West. Our culture
is in feeble touch with its female archetypes, reflected
most seriously in its failure to regard and honour the
mother. She is the figure central to most human societies—around her they organize their spaces, their
buildings, and many of their customs. The West's
chronic inability to deal with its transgression is aggra-
vated by the absence of a guiding female ethos. Excess
—everything too much, except what matters—is allied
to the culture's over-dependence on the male inclination to solve everything by action. A telling counter is
Mary of Bethany, who loses herself in order to *be*, and

thereby is able to lead, to accompany, and to console.

Let us return to the constituent elements. While September 11 does point to action, its gesture is oblique. The fairy-tale path is not the only one. We might take another fundamental fact as our starting point. Washington, at its most effectively powerful, and even with good fortune, is not going to neutralise all the states that back terror; nor is it going to destroy all the terrorist-training camps; nor is it going to stop some states, at present, for instance, North Korea, from manufacturing weapons of mass destruction, including medium- and long-range missiles with nuclear capability. Its moves to seize the assets and freeze the bank accounts of groups linked with al-Qaeda have proved pitifully inadequate, given the size of the world's black economy and the number of unregulated banks and finance intermediaries operating in Pakistan alone, just to take one case. It will prove impossible to root out all the sources of terror.

What follows? One parallel is the madness of sifting mega-tons of Twin Towers' debris for clues. The urge to control on its own will lead to paranoia, fear around every corner—which means imagining threats from every second Middle-Eastern state, every second Muslim citizen, every second bulging suitcase. To be guided solely by reason is to expect the worst. It prescribes that the only path to security is via the superpower ego fighting adversity before emerging triumphant. But the reality is that America will at best make limited progress with terrorism. Pure reason leads into unreason.

We have freed ourselves in the West from ritual—one factor in the emptying of the churches. Our sense of self is no longer tribal, fortified by uniform codes of behaviour and doctrine. Fundamentalist belief and practice may survive on the margins, but it has little resonance in the mainstream culture. September 11 presses us to take the next step, to free ourselves from secular substitutes. We have to detach ourselves from the belief in redemption through decisive action.

The alternative path is that of balance, under the authority of 'nothing too much'. Let me draw on a parallel case of the undermining of the sense of security on which everyday life is usually based. Whilst it is trivial in comparison with the gravity of September 11, it does suggest a useful lesson. In Australia, the greatest material threat to the security of the home, apart from bushfire and burglary, is white ants. These termites nest underground and can tunnel hundreds of metres looking for their staple food—timber. If they happen upon a house, the first sign of their presence is usually crinkling paint on skirting boards. An anxious prod will expose a gaping black hole—all the wood behind has been eaten away. Wooden floors give way under foot, ceilings sag, and panel walls disintegrate. There are cases of people leaving their houses for a fortnight to return to a pile of dust. In Australia, one can buy home-insurance cover for fire, earthquake, flood, cyclone, and war, indeed for any act of man or god—except white ants. Insurance companies have now added a second exemption—terrorism.

The solution that pest exterminators offer is to pump a chemical shield under the building. They will blow arsenic powder into termite channels in the remaining architraves in the hope that it will be carried back to the nest and kill the queen—she breeds tens of thousands of new slave workers each day. The neighbourhood will be scoured for nests. White ants are uncannily similar to al-Qaeda cells in their capacity, when under attack, to segment and disperse in ever-larger numbers.

When, six months later the termites return, the pest exterminator will shrug his shoulders and smile knowingly—in embarrassed sympathy, in philosophical helplessness, in mockery at the curse. In this domain, science is crude, the experts often impotent, and the only solution for the fretful owner is to learn to relax, and to live with the enduring threat to the solidity of the house. It may turn out, after all, that the termites have paid their last visit.

If there is any doubt about the perplexing duality that faces us, a correct reading of the enemy may help. The Usama strategy highlights one of the fundamentals: 'Know thine enemy!' The West's previous battle had been against communism, taking the form of a 40-year 'cold war' punctuated by occasional, limited hot wars. This was a battle of competing materialisms.

Thus it was enough to demonstrate the prodigious superiority of democratic capitalism at generating wealth, its industrial war production at a volume and technical sophistication that could not be matched. The Soviet Union disintegrated from within once it recognised the inevitable—that even by impoverishing and tyrannising its own people it could not keep up. Most communist fellow-travellers in the West had long realised that their dreams of communal utopia were better served, if far from imperfectly, by their own consumer societies.

The enemy of 2001 spoke a different language. He charged the West with unbelief. He asserted that God had created the twin towers of his eternal culture. No hijacked planes could bring them down. He himself has always lived in Spartan austerity, true to his polemic against the profane and decadent enemy. A visitor to this Saudi multi-millionaire's house in Sudan was astonished: 'no fridge, no air conditioning, no fancy car, nothing.' Earlier, in Afghanistan, he had lived with the Arab fighters and Afghan peasants, cooking and eating with them, helping them dig trenches. A range of reports confirm Usama's courage in December 2001, commanding his troops in the Tora Bora region until the last moment, before disappearing on foot towards Pakistan.

The Soviet leadership, consistent with the materialist logic of its confrontation with the industrialised First World, had cushioned itself in billionaire-style luxury

—villas, yachts, mistresses, and plump indolence. Russia's Leonid Brezhnev had bragged to Richard Nixon that he lived far better than the American president. The Chinese communist leadership has followed the same, self-indulgent worldly path.

Usama, as the nemesis of the West, taunted: 'What do *you* believe?' The symbolism of President Bush's response is not encouraging. After ditching the first title for the military campaign, *Operation Infinite Justice*, in embarrassment, the war on terrorism was renamed *Operation Enduring Freedom*. It appears that the Americans were still mentally fighting their previous war, in which the rhetoric of freedom and material progress had been a fitting counter to communism.

They were oblivious to the blueprint. Marlow's flight from the absurd city is not in search of freedom—the modern individual has plenty of that. From Marlow's perspective, the Thomas Jefferson who wrote the American *Declaration of Independence* was an irrelevancy, a bore. The words are beautiful on the outside:

> We hold these truths to be self-evident, that all men are created equal, that they are endowed by their Creator with certain inalienable Rights, that among these are Life, Liberty and the pursuit of Happiness.

In practice, the Jefferson ideal is dreamland happiness, with nothing left to say to the modern West. The Statue of Liberty is an obsolete symbol, its gesture of no relevance to the metaphysical quest. Imagine Marlow's scorn, were his journey into the heart of darkness, or the journey up the Mekong River in the film *Apocalypse Now*, or the striving for male initiation in *Fight Club* to be turned into a soap opera titled *Operation Enduring Freedom*!

Also lost in the logic of the last war were critics of President Bush from the political left. They argued, as we have seen, that America was growing ever richer at the expense of the under-developed world. Its indifference and greed were generating resentment among the suffering masses in poorer countries — the major cause of the new terrorism. This argument fails on two counts. First, it is false. A Saudi multi-millionaire hardly belongs among the wretched of the earth, nor do his technocrat lieutenants, nor do typical al-Qaeda members from, to take one example, Singapore — who, according to former prime minister Lee Kuan Yew, enjoy well-off Western lifestyles. Second, it misreads a metaphysical crisis as moral.

A quite different matter is the responsibility of a civilization based on excess towards the rest of the world. We shall know our character has found some poise only when all the societies of the West become generous with their practical knowledge and their wealth — to less well-off tenants of our shared earth. Following the example of Mary of Bethany, this means giving for the sake of giving; service for the sake of service. And there is warning that any expectation of reward will corrupt the ethos. We have enough.

Usama bin Laden cannot be answered by the *Ikea* apartment, doctrines of universal human values, and the inalienable right to the pursuit of happiness — nor by what has accompanied them, mute dread in the face of death. Moreover, the Pied Piper of holy war played a tune that the leaders of the West, those with the power of both decision-making and opinion, the modern mayors of Hamelin, were in danger of misreading. They fell for the illusion that he piped solely to the rats of his own cultural domain. This led them to the conclusion that if they succeeded in killing the rats all would be well. In fact, the children of the West, weeping over Lazarus, were themselves under threat, and from a tune that was not new to their ears.

Altogether, we have been plunged into a sea of difficulty utterly beyond our conception. Our preparation could not have been worse — a half-century Golden Age of comfortable, oblivious excess. Our identification has been with Lazarus, and with his cry to be given more of this blind, stumbling, package-tour life. It has not been with his changed sister, Mary. Our departure from the absurd city, like Marlow's, has been heedlessly casual, and in spite of the shock. Like him, we have ended up in a nightmare of fathomless profundity. For most of the time we still pretend it is not happening.

The *long haul* is both a practical reality and a psychic metaphor. What in actuality can the American government do? A worldwide terrorist network confronts it, one that is invisible, its cells based in dozens of countries across all five continents, perhaps proliferating like white ants — our Intelligence simply does not know. To single out Iraq appears more like an excuse for doing something, a sideshow to release pressure. That scenario is opposite to the preceding one, of a successfully prosecuted Afghan war. This time the justification is loose, the risks large, and the potential gains modest. Meanwhile dangers multiply, and modest gains are likely to be the best we are going to get.

Gunaratna puts it that America and its allies are going to have to learn how to fight on the run, improvising, learning as they go — against this entirely new type of elusive, global enemy. Such a long, slow, bit-by-bit haul will require supreme resources of intelligence, diplomacy, and tactical strike-power, in combination with the character virtues of patience, perseverance, and stoicism.

The United States government, under threat of paralysis, has to keep moving in awesomely difficult circumstances. The response of everyone else in the West, whatever their misgivings about American society, should be simple. Out of naked self-interest, let alone empathy, they should be wishing President Bush and his administration good judgment and good fortune.

We are all responsible. We have drunk in the excess and indulged in the comfort. Equally, we are the heirs of a long and rich culture. The seriousness of the condition into which we have been cast demands that we all wake up from our day-to-day oblivion, and focus on the reality. Responsibility means that everybody is cast in the role of the ideal captain who has to steer the ship of state under threat—the boy who has grown up. Such is the inclusive virtue of democracy at its best. This is the person who accepts the weight of making decisions that affect the lives of many citizens, who is unblinkingly alert to the potential for dire consequences, is willing to take responsibility for them, and then, at the end of it all, remains able to act.

The West's own formative story of the hero, Homer's *Iliad*, teaches a key lesson about detachment. Achilles is the quintessential man of action, a warrior so superior to all others who fight the Trojan War that the storyteller chooses two recurring adjectives— 'godlike' and 'man-slaughtering'. Yet this hero only becomes great after the action, in the twilight hours of reflection. Grief-stricken at the death of his friend, disconnected from his own glory, brooding over the sense of it all, he weeps with the enemy king, whom he honours as his guest, welcoming him: 'Aged, magnificent Sir!' These best two of men, each of who has ruined the other's life, treat one another with courtesy, and share the unbearable weight of the human condition. Jesus would not have snorted angrily at their weeping.

Achilles had great presence earlier, when he stood unarmed next to the Greek defences, three times bellowing his great war cry, and the Trojan army shivered at the sight of his flaming head encircled by a golden cloud. Yet this is not the complete man; his charisma here was dependent on an external agent, a goddess bathing him in light. He is not the man we remember.

The climax to *The Iliad*, the story with which the high culture of the West begins, Homer's teaching, concerns the man who grieves with the enemy king. His pride and desire, his formidable ego, have all turned to dust—devoured by suffering. In his own mind, his deeds have become as worthy as the child's demolished sandcastle.

It is this world-weary, twilight Achilles whose being shines eternally over the plains of Troy, over the West's cultural future, and in its memory. He is a being huge and radiant, adamant in his poise, an exemplar of what it is to be human. He can truly assert, now that he is indifferent to all self-proclamation: 'I am!' Achilles answers *Heart of Darkness*.

The right path may lead us further into tragedy. It did with Achilles, due to his rampaging fury in battle, his pitiless killing of innocent youths, his defiling of the enemy hero's corpse—just as the Americans would mistreat captured Taliban fighters after their Afghan success. Achilles, once the battle was over, and he had cooled down, accepted responsibility for the horror of his Kurtz self and what it, in its excess, had done. He faced, clear and straight, the absurdity of his glory. Beyond the need for further action, or for intoxicants, he found poise within. And thereby he restored a greater order.

The task today, as always for the hero, centres on *being*. The opening mode in our current situation is again through doing—but doing in order to *be*. Ride into battle, yes, deploying every resource, material and mental, at the West's disposal, to counter the terrorist threat. This is the great warrior, shining in his magnificence, bellowing at the enemy. Achilles, true to his vocation, that of warrior, plays a vital role in his people, the Greeks, winning the Trojan War. Do what has to be done, and with no holding back. But do it with detachment. Do not expect that a guiding shape will be provided from outside the self—such as we all, in our weakness, seek. *Being* is a matter of presence in the here and now.

Little is as it was before September 11. Apollo joins 'Nothing in excess!' to 'Know thyself!' Here are the twin towers of our culture. We have denied the ancestral god. We imagined we could do it on our own, without help or guidance, our backs turned on our old wisdoms. So we built a civilization symbolised by the skyscraper: a soaring steel-and-concrete infinitude, yesterday 110 storeys high; tomorrow, 220. That order is past.

What remains, on the brink of folly, is a hole of vast discomposure. We have been thrown back on our ancient authorities. There is nothing else, apart from ourselves. The god of light has returned. His instruction to us is that balance depends on self-inquiry. Only when we have travelled within — to the true Inner Station — might we start to rise.

Let us then, in a spirit of humility and reverence, retrace the journey that we — and, with us, our culture — have unwittingly taken. There is no other way to find where we have arrived, and what might be in store. In any case, we have no choice. In our recently departed self, cast as Joseph Conrad's Marlow, we steamed up the wrong river. This time, September 11, 2001 is our appointed guide. This time, things are so grave as to be beyond the domain of good and evil.

ACKNOWLEDGMENTS

This book has been assisted in a range of ways, from the generous donation of scholarly and technical expertise to the benefit I have gained from more general discussions. I wish to thank Wendy Bowler, Stephen Crittenden, Rohan Gunaratna, Michael Leunig, William Maley, Alan Parkinson, Tony Pagliaro, Michael Roux, Edgar Smith, and Hugh White. I am especially grateful to Sally Warhaft, Mike Richards, and Scribe's publisher, Henry Rosenbloom.